**DO NOT REMOVE
CARDS FROM POCKET**

DAVE
BARRY
TURNS
40

ALSO BY DAVE BARRY

The Taming of the Screw
Babies and Other Hazards of Sex
Stay Fit and Healthy Until You're Dead
Claw Your Way to the Top
Bad Habits
Dave Barry's Guide to Marriage and/or Sex
Homes and Other Black Holes
Dave Barry's Greatest Hits
Dave Barry Slept Here

DAVE BARRY TURNS 40

CROWN PUBLISHERS, INC. NEW YORK

PUBLISHED BY CROWN PUBLISHERS, INC., 201 EAST 50TH STREET, NEW YORK, NEW YORK 10022

BOOK DESIGN BY KATHY KIKKERT

CROWN IS A TRADEMARK OF CROWN PUBLISHERS, INC.

MANUFACTURED IN THE UNITED STATES OF AMERICA

LIBRARY OF CONGRESS CATALOGING-IN-PUBLICATION DATA

BARRY, DAVE.
DAVE BARRY TURNS 40 / DAVE BARRY.
1. AGING—HUMOR.   2. MIDLIFE CRISIS—HUMOR.   I. TITLE.
PN6231.A43B37   1990
818′.5402—DC20
90-1621

ISBN 0-517-57755-0

10   9   8   7   6   5   4   3   2   1

FIRST EDITION

For Dan Quayle,
who proved to my generation that,
frankly, **anybody** *can make it*

CONTENTS

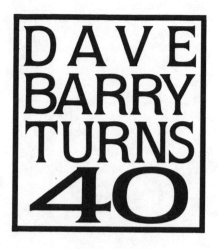

INTRODUCTION

Well, it's finally happening. I'm talking about the long-predicted Aging Process. I see many signs of it in my own life. For example, I have become tremendously concerned about my gums. There was a time when I could go for *decades* without thinking about my gums, but recently they have come to loom far larger in my mind than the Greenhouse Effect.

Also, young people I meet keep using the word "Mister," causing me to whirl around and look behind me, expecting to see somebody with whom I associate this title, such as the Pope or Walter Cronkite, only to realize that these young people are talking to *me.*

Also, if I attempt to throw a softball without carefully warming up, I have to wait until approximately the next presidential administration before I can attempt to do this again.

Also, I have long, animated conversations with my friends—friends with whom I used to ingest banned substances and swim naked—on the importance of dietary fiber.

Also, I find myself asking my son, in a solemn parental

1

voice, the same profoundly stupid old-fogey questions that my parents used to ask me, such as: "Do you want to poke somebody's *eye* out?"

Also—this is most terrifying—I sometimes catch myself humming along to elevator music.

Of course I'm not alone. Growing older is a Major Lifestyle Trend, potentially even bigger than cable television. Millions of us, the entire legendary Baby Boom herd of Mouseketeer-watching, Hula-Hoop-spinning, Beatles-admiring, hair-growing, pot-smoking, funky-chicken-dancing, lovemaking, résumé-writing, career-pursuing, insurance-buying, fitness-obsessing, Lamaze-class-taking, breast-feeding, data-processing, mortgage-paying, Parents'-Night-attending, business-card-exchanging, compact-disc-owning, tooth-flossing individuals, are lunging toward:

$\longrightarrow$ MIDDLE AGE $\longleftarrow$

Yes. Say it out loud, Boomers: We are MIDDLE-AGED. The time has come for us to stop identifying with Wally and The Beav; we are now a *lot* closer to Ward and June. *Somebody* has to be the grownups, and now it's our turn.

The problem is, I'm not sure we're ready. I've been hanging around with people roughly my own age for the bulk of my life, and I frankly do not feel that, as a group, we have acquired the wisdom and maturity needed to run the world, or even necessarily power tools. Many of us, I'm convinced, only *look* like grownups.

For example, I work for a newspaper Sunday magazine whose staff consists mostly of people about my age. If

2

you happened to visit us briefly from the outside world, we'd strike you as being regular middle-aged guys with ties and desks and families and various degrees of hair loss. "Huh!" you'd say. "This is a group of adults charged with putting out a magazine under constant deadline pressure! They must be very responsible!" Then you'd leave, and we'd resume playing chairball, a game we invented one day in the conference room while attempting to hold a conference, in which the players scuttle violently around on rolling chairs, trying to throw a foam-rubber ball through a hoop up on the wall.

I don't mean to suggest that all we do, at the office, is play chairball. Sometimes we throw the Frisbee. Sometimes we practice our juggling. Sometimes we even put out the magazine, but you would never conclude, if you secretly observed us for several weeks, that this was anywhere near our highest priority.

And I don't think it's just me and my co-workers who do stuff like this. I think the entire Baby Boom generation is having trouble letting go of the idea that it represents The Nation's Youth and has an inalienable right to be wild and carefree. The whole Iran-contra scandal, in my opinion, basically boiled down to some fortyish guys in the White House basement playing an international top-secret multimillion-dollar version of chairball.

This is why I'm alarmed at the prospect of somebody my age getting into the Oval Office. Because I know that if *I* got in there, I'd probably be okay for the first few days, but then I'd do something to amuse myself, such as order the Marines to invade Cleveland, or issue a proclamation honoring Nasal Discharge Week, or leave a prank message on the Hot Phone answering machine ("Thanks for calling the White House. We can't recall our bombers right now, but if you leave your name and the time you called . . .").

But the alarming truth is, people my age *are* taking over the government, along with almost everything else. And what is even more terrifying, I'm seeing more and more important jobs being done by people who are even *younger* than I am. The scariest example is doctors. If you wake up from a terrible accident to find yourself strapped down on your back in an operating room awaiting emergency surgery, and a person walks in who is about to open you up with a sharp implement and root around among your personal organs, you want this person to look as much as possible like Robert Young, right? Well, today the odds are that you're going to look up and see Sean Penn.

And let's talk about airline pilots. I have long felt that if I'm going to risk my life and valuable carry-on belongings in a profoundly heavy machine going absurdly fast way the hell up in the air over places such as Arkansas, where I don't even know anybody, then I want whoever is operating this machine to be *much* older and more mature than I. But now I routinely get on planes where the entire flight crew looks like it's raising money for its Class Trip. I am very nervous on these flights. I want the crew to leave the cockpit door open so I can make sure they're not using the navigational computer to play Death Blasters from Planet Doom.

I'm not suggesting that anything can be done about this trend. I mean, we can't pass a law requiring, for example, that airline pilots always have to be older than we are. That could become a real problem once we started reaching, say, our eighties ("This is your captain, and my name is, um . . . it's . . . my name is right on the tip of my tongue . . .").

No, the only solution is for us to face up to the fact that we are no longer the Hope for the Future. The Hope for the Future now consists of the kids who like to shave their heads and ride skateboards off the tops of buildings. We Baby Boomers are the Hope for Right Now, and we're going to have to accept it.

Which is why I wrote this book. My goal is to explore all the ramifications—physiological, emotional, and social—of turning 40, in hopes that, by improving our understanding and awareness of the true significance of this challenging and extremely important new phase in our lives, we will acquire, as countless generations have acquired before us, the wisdom, vision, and maturity we need to assume our rightful responsibilities and obligations as the moral, intellectual, political, and spiritual leaders—and, yes, caretakers—of this increasingly fragile planet.

Then let's drink a bunch of beer and set off fireworks.

1

ARE YOU A GROWNUP YET? A SCIENTIFIC QUIZ

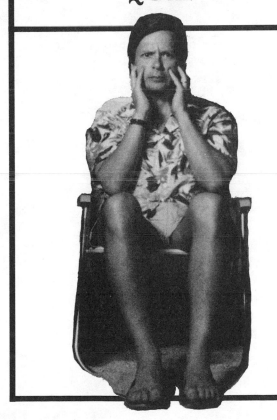

This quiz is designed to help you get a handle on how far you have progressed toward becoming a grownup, as measured by the Standardized Psychological Maturity Scale, which assesses your maturity level on a scale of zero (Very Immature) to ten (Legally Dead). Answer the questions below as honestly as you can, bearing in mind that there are no "right" or "wrong" answers. Our goal, in this exercise, is not to judge you according to someone else's arbitrary system of values. Our goal is to waste time.

1. If another driver cuts you off in traffic, you will:
   a. Keep your temper firmly in check, because nobody wins when you "play games" with Traffic Safety.
   b. Honk your horn in an irritated fashion and possibly even make a famous hand gesture.
   c. Dedicate yourself totally to gaining automotive revenge—no matter what the risk to property or human life—by *cutting the other driver off,* even if this means drastically altering your plans and, if necessary, following him to Mexico.

2. When you participate in a friendly, informal,
   meaningless pickup game such as volleyball or
   softball, you play at an intensity level that would be
   appropriate for:
   a. A friendly, informal, meaningless pickup game.
   b. The Olympic finals.
   c. Iwo Jima.
3. You generally leave parties:
   a. Well before all the other guests have left.
   b. When there are only one or two other guests
   remaining.
   c. At gunpoint.
4. What do you do when the song "Jumpin' Jack
   Flash," by the Rolling Stones, comes on your car
   radio?
   a. You turn it off and call the office on your car
   phone to see if any of your business associates
   have tried to reach you on *their* car phones.
   b. You change to a "mellow rock" station oriented
   toward sensitive songs such as "Feelin' Groovy"
   from Simon and Garfunkel's early years ("The
   Weenie Period"), played by disc jockeys who are
   so low-key that they take Quaaludes to *wake up*.
   c. You crank the radio volume all the way up and
   do the Car Dance, wherein you bounce your butt
   rhythmically on the seat, and you sing along with
   Mick Jagger using the cigarette lighter as a
   microphone while gradually pressing down harder
   and harder on the accelerator, so that when you
   get to the part where you and Mick sing that
   "Jumpin' Jack Flash is a GAS GAS GAS," you are

going at least eighty-five miles per hour, even inside your garage.

5. If it were entirely up to you to feed yourself, your diet would consist of:
   a. Fruits, vegetables, and low-cholesterol protein sources.
   b. Fried foods and frozen dinners.
   c. Milk Duds.

6. In conversations with your co-workers, how do you refer to your boss?
   a. "Mr. Druckerman."
   b. "Ted."
   c. "The Human Hemorrhoid."

7. If you have any money left after you take care of basic living expenses, you put it into:
   a. A diversified investment portfolio with emphasis on proven equities offering secure long-term growth potential.
   b. Paying off your Visa bill.
   c. Skee-ball.

8. You are in a very important, very serious corporate meeting attended by major, high-level officers. During a momentary silence, one of the participants—the chief executive officer of a firm that your company desperately wants to win as a client—emits a brief but fabric-rendingly-loud burst of flatulence. What do you do?
   a. Act as though absolutely nothing has happened.
   b. Titter involuntarily, but quickly regain your composure.
   c. Lunge for the 179-page market survey report in

front of you and hide your face behind it and
make a desperate but clearly hopeless effort to
remain silent while your body vibrates with
pent-up laughter that finally erupts with a violent,
wet gasping noise like several dozen whales
surfacing simultaneously, accompanied by a
rivulet of fast-moving drool trickling out from
under the report and making its away across the
conference table and finally dribbling into the lap
of the potential client's attorney, at which point
you emerge from behind the report and attempt
to apologize to seventeen stony, staring corporate
faces, who unfortunately serve only to remind you
of the awesome, nearly life-threatening *humor* of
the situation, so that all you can say to them—to
the people who hold your professional future in
their hands—is, quote, "WHOOOOO," after
which you pull your head, turtle-like, back into
the report, and the only noise in the conference
room, aside from the labored, gurgling gasps that
you continue to emit, is the sound of the
potential client picking up his briefcase and
marching grimly and permanently from the room.

9. Your taste in the performing arts runs toward:
   a. Ballet, opera, classical music.
   b. Television, movies, pop concerts.
   c. Booger jokes.

10. If you had just acquired a puppy, your highest
   priority, in terms of discipline, would be training
   it to:
   a. Heel.

b. Roll over.

c. Pee on the Amway distributor.

How to Score First off, you have to make the woman believe that you really *care* about her as a person, and then you . . .

Whoops! Sorry! Wrong kind of scoring! To score yourself on the maturity quiz, give yourself one point for each "A" answer, half a point for each "B" answer, and zero points for each "C" answer, then total up your points. If you actually take the trouble to *do* this, you are a fairly mature person. A lot of us are already reading the next chapter.

YOUR
DISINTEGRATING
BODY

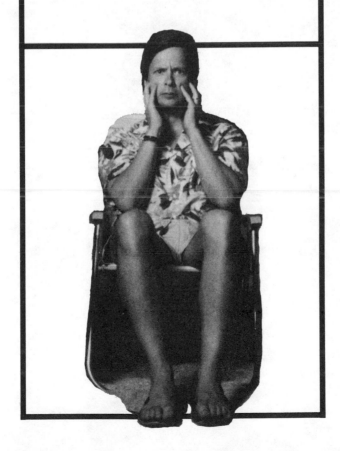

O

ne of the more trau-
matic aspects of reaching age 40 is the realization that you no longer have the same body you had when you were 21. I know *I* don't. Sometimes when I take a shower I look down at my body and I want to scream: "Hey, THIS isn't my body! THIS body belongs to Willard Scott!"

But this is perfectly natural. Screaming in the shower, I mean. Reaching age 40, however, is NOT natural. I base this statement on extensive scientific documentation in the form of a newspaper article I vaguely remember reading once, which stated that the life expectancy for human beings in the wild is about 35 years. Think about what that means. It means that if you were in the wild, even in the nonsmoking section, by now you'd be Worm Chow. So we can clearly see that going past age 40 is basically an affront to Nature, with Exhibit A being the Gabor sisters.

Nevertheless, we *are* living longer. Thanks to modern medical advances such as antibiotics, nasal spray, and Diet Coke, it has become quite routine for people in the civilized world to pass the age of 40, sometimes more than once. As a person reaching this milestone, you need to take the time to learn about the biological changes that are taking place within your body, so that you will be better able to understand and cope with the inevitable and completely natural elements of the aging process—the minor aches, pains, dental problems, intestinal malfunctions, muscle deterioration, emotional instability, memory lapses, hearing and vision loss, impotence, seizures, growths, prostate problems, greatly reduced limb function, massive coronary failure, death, and, of course, painful hemorrhoidal swelling—that make up this exciting adventure we call "middle age."

My goal, in this chapter, is to explore these topics in as much detail as possible without doing any actual research, in the hopes that when I am done, you will have the knowledge you need to develop healthier lifestyle habits. For example, right now you may be the kind of person who goes to a restaurant and, without thinking, orders a great big juicy steak. My hope is that, after reading this chapter and becoming aware of the dangers of ingesting high-cholesterol foods, you will also order a martini the size of Lake Huron. Remember the words of the wise old Health Proverb: "A person who observes the rules of proper nutrition is a person who should never be placed in charge of a barbecue."

But enough inspiration. It's time to put on our protective eyewear and take a detailed, probing look inside your increasingly Spam-like body, starting with a factual overview of:

THE AGING PROCESS

Why do we get older? Why do our bodies wear out? Why can't we just go on and on and on, accumulating a potentially infinite number of Frequent Flier mileage points? These are the kinds of questions that philosophers have been asking ever since they realized that being a philosopher did not involve any heavy lifting.

And yet the answer is really very simple: Our bodies are mechanical devices, and like all mechanical devices, they break down. Some devices, such as battery-operated toys costing $39.95, break down almost instantly upon exposure to the Earth's atmosphere. Other devices, such as stereo systems owned by your next-door neighbors' 13-year-old son who likes to listen to bands with names like "Nerve Damage" at a volume capable of disintegrating limestone, will continue to function perfectly for many years, even if you hit them with an ax. But the fundamental law of physics is that sooner or later every mechanism ceases to function for one reason or another, and it is never covered under the warranty.

As we know from slicing up dead worms in Biology Lab, the "parts" that make up this miraculous "mechanism" that we call the human body are called "cells"— billions and billions (even more, in the case of Marlon Brando) of organisms so tiny that we cannot see or hear them unless we have been using illegal narcotics. When you are very young, each of your cells, based on its individual personality and aptitude, selects an area of specialization, such as the thigh, in which to pursue its career. As you grow, the cell multiplies, and it teaches its offspring to be thigh cells also, showing them the various "tricks of the trade." Thus the proud thigh-cell tradition is handed down from generation to generation, so that by the time you're a teenager, you have an extremely competent, efficient, and hard-working colony down there, providing you with thighs so sleek and taut that they look great even when encased in Spandex garments that would be a snug fit on a Bic pen. But as your body approaches middle age, this cellular discipline starts to break down. The newer cells—you know how it is with the young—start to challenge the conventional values of their elders. "What's so great about sleek and taut?" is what these newer cells would say, if they had mouths, which thank God they do not. They become listless and bored, and many of them, looking for "kicks," turn to cellulite. Your bodily tissue begins to deteriorate, gradually becoming saggier and lumpier, until one day you glance in the mirror and realize, to your horror, that you look as though for some reason you are attempting to smuggle out of the country an entire driveway's worth of gravel concealed inside your upper legs.

And this very same process is going on *all over your body.*

Is there something you can do about it? You're darned right there is! You *can* fight back. Mister Old Age is not going to get *you,* by golly! All you need is a little determination—a willingness to get out of that reclining lounge chair, climb into that sweatsuit, lace on those running shoes, stride out that front door, and *hurl yourself in front of that municipal bus.*

No, wait. Sorry. For a moment there I got a carried

away by the bleakness of it all. Forget what I said. Really. There is absolutely no need to become suicidally depressed about the fact that every organ in your body is headed straight down the biological toilet. There really *are* things that you can do to keep your body looking healthy and youthful for years to come. But before I discuss these things, I want you to answer the following questions honestly: Are you willing to make the hard sacrifices needed to be *really* healthy? Are you willing to commit yourself *totally* to a program of regular exercise, close medical supervision, and the elimination of all caffeine, alcohol, and rich foods, to be replaced by a strict diet of nutrition-rich, kelp-like plant growths so unappetizing that they will make you actually lust for tofu? Or are you the kind of shallow, irresponsible person who wants a purely cosmetic change, a "quick and dirty" surface gloss that may make you *look* young and healthy, but actually has no long-term value? Me too.

LIPOSUCTION

A few people—and I see no reason why we should not beat them to death with sticks—manage to reach middle age with lean, slender bodies. But most of us, by the time we turn 40, contain large sectors of fatty tissue, living memorials to every high-calorie item we have ever consumed—every brownie, ice cream cone, Milky Way, Chuckle, Eskimo Pie, Sno-Ball, and Twinkie. Every jelly bean, Frosted Flake, and potato chip. *Every single M&M.* It's all still there. Your body is convinced that you're going to need it someday, that the only thing standing between you and starvation will be the stored fat from a Ring Ding you ate in second grade.

This is stupid, of course. Now that we have refrigerators, there is no longer any need to use the human buttock as a food-storage device. But try getting this message through to your body. Try leaning back over your shoulder and shouting at your buttocks: "HEY BACK THERE! STOP STORING FAT!" See if you get anywhere. If you do, let me know. I'll try anything that does not require actually eating less.

In fact, many of us are willing to consider extreme measures to become slimmer. I bet that more than once, when nobody was around, you've grabbed a handful of your fat and wished something truly ridiculous, something like: "I wish some doctor would just stick a tube into my body and turn on a pump and *suck this fat right out.*" Ha ha! You crazy nut! What a wacky idea! Do you honestly think, with all the serious medical problems confronting the human race, that a physician—a person who has gone through long, grueling years of medical training in order to acquire vital healing skills that could be used to make a real difference in the lives of suffering people—do you honestly think that such a person would use this precious ability to suck bacon cheeseburgers out of your thighs?

Well, certainly not for *free.* No sir, it could run you more than a thousand buckeroos per thigh. This is not because the liposuction procedure itself is difficult. The procedure itself could be performed flawlessly by anyone who has completed the basic training course at Roto-Rooter. What makes it expensive is the problem of *what to do with your fat.* Think about it. You know from personal experience that your fat is the most malevolent, indestructible substance on the planet. There is no way to kill it. You've tried starving it, stretching it, cursing at it, pummeling it, and squeezing it into foundation garments, yet nothing has had the slightest effect. So it is very tough, and it is also going to be *very angry* that it has been unceremoniously sucked out of your body. The liposuction clinic cannot simply throw this dangerous substance into the garbage can. It would escape and follow you home. Even if you moved across the country and got a whole new identity, your fat would *track you down,* and one day when you least expected it, probably at a swimming pool, it would pounce upon you and bloat your butt up to the size of a postal facility.

For this reason, every liposuction clinic is required to maintain, at great expense, a Maximum Security Fat Prison where the contents removed from patients are incarcerated under twenty-four-hour armed guard. Unfortunately, as liposuction becomes increasingly popular, these facilities have become more and more overcrowded, and unless something is done soon, we are going to see a tragic incident wherein a medical professional building is rocked by the unmistakable sound ("Splooosh") of high-pressure liposuction by-products exploding through steel doors, followed by the dreaded, revenge-seeking Wall of Fat surging down once-quiet suburban streets and engulfing innocent civilians. But other than that, there are few side effects.

Another very popular form of anti-aging cosmetic surgery is, of course:

THE FACELIFT

This is the procedure wherein the plastic surgeon perks up your face by standing behind you, pulling your skin back on both sides of your head until the front is nice and tight, and then attaching the flaps of excess skin to the back of your head with a staple gun. Sure it stings, but the visual effect is stunning, as you are miraculously transformed from a person with bags and wrinkles into a person whose eyes appear to be just slightly too far apart. In fact, if you get repeated facelifts, your eyes will gradually migrate around to the side of your head, carp-like, and you will experience a real bonus in the peripheral-vision department.

But the above are only two of the many cosmetic-surgery possibilities. Great strides forward are being made in this exciting field as the medical community becomes increasingly aware of the benefits, both psychological and physical, of getting rich. One popular new technique is called lipografting, or "fat recycling," wherein fat cells are removed from one part of your body that is too large, such as your buttocks, and injected into an area where you wish to have added fullness, such as your lips; people will then be literally kissing your ass.

Ha ha! That was just a small example of lipografting humor, to give you a sense of the happy, upbeat spirit that pervades this fast-growing field. And the best is yet to come. Someday, within your lifetime, it may be possible for a plastic surgeon to attach a tube to you and, using a very powerful pump, slurp up *your entire body* and replace it with that of a scientifically selected teenager.

Of course this would raise serious ethical questions, such as how many exemptions you could claim on your income tax. But I am confident that we will one day be able to solve problems like this, which is a lot more than I can say for the problem of:

MALE PATTERN BALDNESS

Let me begin this very sensitive discussion by stating that I see *nothing funny* about baldness. The fact that I, personally, have reached age 42 without any significant hair loss does NOT mean that I have the right to make insensitive remarks about those of you whose heads are turning into Mosquito Landing Zones.

Actually, massive hair loss is not the tragedy that many men make it out to be. There are countless examples of men who actually look *better* without hair. The late Yul Brynner springs immediately to mind. Also there was what's-his-name, the guy who was in *The Magnificent Seven*. No, wait, that was also the late Yul Brynner. Hmmmmm.

Well, I'm certain that there are many examples of nondeceased men who look better bald, but quite frankly I cannot afford to spend the next decade trying to think of their names. The point is that going bald is a *perfectly natural* part of the aging process, like having all your teeth rot and fall out, and there is no reason to be self-conscious about it and assume that your co-workers are always staring at the top of your head and snickering behind your back. Sometimes they actually laugh out loud.

No! I'm just kidding! Really, I'm sure everybody is getting used to your head. However, if you're really bothered by your hair loss, there *are* various techniques that you can employ to combat it. And although these techniques vary greatly in cost and degree of medical risk, each of them, if used correctly, can enable the man who's getting a little "thin on top" to turn himself into a man who looks "silly."

The method preferred by most balding men for making themselves look silly is called the "comb-over," which is when the man grows the hair on one side of his head very long and combs it across the bald area, creating an effect that looks very realistic and natural to observers who have been blind since birth. To everyone else, it looks like hair being combed over a bald area, which is usually clearly visible through the hair strands, so that from the top, the head looks like an egg in the grasp of a large tropical spider. Comb-over users with large balding areas have to get the hair from far down on the sides of their heads, which means they must part their hair comically low, sometimes around the ear. You will see men who are basically trying to cover their entire skulls with one gigantic Sideburn From Hell. It's definitely an "eye-catching" look, men! Trust me!

Another option, of course, is to wear a hairpiece. Famous actor and stud muffin Burt Reynolds wears one, and he looks terrific; there's no reason why you can't do the same thing.

Of course, when I say "do the same thing," I mean: "Wear Burt Reynolds's hairpiece." This is definitely your best bet, because Burt spends as much money for his hairpiece as most people spend on their dream retirement homes. A hairpiece that costs any less—the kind *you* could afford, for example—is inevitably going to make you look as though you have for some reason decided to glue a road-kill to your scalp. Which is not entirely a bad thing. Ludicrously obvious hairpieces serve as an important source of harmless entertainment for society in general. My wife and I and another couple were once entertained for an entire seven-hour plane flight by two men, traveling together, who were both wearing toupees that would have been detectable from outside the solar system. Apparently they were on their way to the international convention of the Bad Hairpiece Club. We made numerous unnecessary trips to the lavatory so that we could view these men from various angles at close range. It was such fun that we felt like applauding them as they got off the plane. We wanted to find out if they were available for weddings, bar mitzvahs, etc. So there you have one true-life example of how a hairpiece can really change the way people look at you. Kind of sideways, is how we did it.

A more extreme option for balding men is to have "plugs" of hair removed from somewhere else on your body and transplanted to your head, where they take root and, over the course of time, come to look like plugs of hair transplanted from somewhere else. And here's an exciting piece of news: There is now a miraculous new product, available by prescription, that can actually *reverse* a certain specific type of male-pattern baldness that, needless to say, is not the same as yours!

So the bottom line, guys, is that there are many positive avenues for you to pursue. My only advice would be, don't become obsessive about your baldness. It's really no big deal. And there's no reason for you to be jealous of guys like me, guys with more hair than they know what to do with, guys who can run their hands through their hair and feel the luxurious . . . Hey, what's this? What's this little empty patch? HEY, WAIT A MINUTE!!

TEETH

What teeth? That is the question. Oh sure, it *looks* like you have teeth, but in fact the dental profession, working gradually so you would not notice, has over the years ground large sectors of your natural teeth into powder, which you then obligingly spit down the little dental toilet. Your mouth is now a whole menagerie of toothlike objects and dental contraptions installed at various times dating back to the Eisenhower administration, a house of dental cards that you know could collapse if you made one wrong bite. Dental tragedies are common among middle-aged people. They'll stop in mid-chew and start thrusting their tongues around, seeking to assess the severity of the damage, knowing that they'll have to make an emergency visit to the dentist, who will, in accordance with the Dental Professionals' Code of Conduct, explain that the only thing to do is grind still *more* sectors of natural tooth into powder and install *more* contraptions that are, judging from the price, made of plutonium. Or maybe the dentist, if he is feeling hostile, will decide to do a "root canal," so called because he uses a special dental backhoe to create a trench in your gum tissue large enough for barge traffic.

This wasn't supposed to happen to us. We were the generation that had Fluoride the Wonder Ingredient in our water supply. We were the generation that was taught the importance of brushing after every meal and getting regular checkups and shrieking, "Look, Mom! No cavities!" We watched Ipana toothpaste commercials starring Bucky Beaver. We watched Colgate commercials where the little smiling tooth knocked out Mister Tooth Decay. We watched Gleem commercials where the baseball player threw a ball at the announcer, but it bounced right off the Invisible Protective Shield made from "Gardol," a substance that could also, as I recall, deflect *machine-gun bullets,* in case somebody ever fired some at your teeth.

So for years we brushed and brushed, and then one day the dental profession announced that, sorry, there had been a mistake. The problem was not Mister Tooth Decay: the problem was Mister Tartar and his evil sidekick Mister Plaque, and it didn't matter *how* much we brushed, because now we all had gum disease, the only treatment for which is to (surprise!) grind additional teeth into powder.

So now many of us have taken up flossing, wherein each night we savagely assault our own gum tissue and stagger off to bed with blood dribbling from our mouths, looking like losing boxers. But we know we're only fooling ourselves. We know that in a few years the dental profession will announce that, sorry, the real problem is not tartar or plaque: The *real* problem is something called "mouth scunge," and the only way to kill it is to heat your teeth to 1,700 degrees with a special home dental laser device after every meal. And even if you do that, it will probably be necessary to locate, via microscope, any of your remaining natural teeth and grind them into powder. In fact, as our life spans increase, the dental professional will eventually run out of teeth, and will have to start grinding away at our skulls. By the year 2010, the average person of your age who has received regular professional dental care will have a head the size of a walnut.

Okay, you can rinse now.

EYES

If you're like most people, as you enter your forties you'll start to become "farsighted," which simply means that you won't be able to read any document located within your immediate Zip Code. The solution is to wear "bifocals," which are a special kind of eyeglasses that somehow make the world look *different,* but not any *clearer.* The best angle for looking through bifocals is when you lean way back and look through the lens bottoms, thus affording the public a spectacular panoramic view of your nasal passages; although a lot of people also get good results by wearing their bifocals up on their foreheads, thus allowing the light rays to bypass the eyeballs altogether and penetrate the brain directly.

FINAL PIECE OF HEALTH ADVICE FOR PEOPLE TURNING 40

You should definitely schedule a thorough medical checkup. Notice I say "schedule." I do not advise that you actually *submit* to a thorough medical checkup, because when you reach age 40 the medical profession suddenly develops an intense interest in a bodily region that I will not name here except to say that the procedure for examining it is so humiliating that even if the doctor says you're perfectly healthy, you will probably want to kill yourself.

Also, you should learn to recognize the various warning signs of heart attack, such as that you feel sharp chest pains or dizziness, or certain familiar printed words suddenly start to appear difoonable and remulatious weedle volcrantitude understand them. That is definitely the time to get help.

3

BEAUTY TIPS FOR THE MORE MATURE GAL (OR, DON'T DISCARD THOSE GROCERY BAGS!)

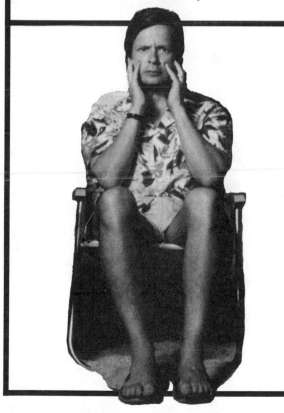

One of the wonderful things about being a woman reaching middle age in the 1990s is that, having grown up during the era of women's liberation, you do not foolishly allow yourself to be constrained by mindless outdated sexist stereotypical notions of what "beauty" is. Right, women? *You* don't feel insecure about growing older! If you glance in the mirror and happen to notice that you've developed crow's-feet formations the size of the Mekong River Delta, you just laugh gaily and say, "Thank goodness I do not foolishly allow myself to be constrained by mindless outdated sexist stereotypical notions of waaaaaaaaAAAAAAAHHHH (sob) (choke) (sound of wrists being slit)." Because let's not kid ourselves: Modern women are no more free from stereotypical notions about beauty than modern men are free from the primal male belief that if you let another male cut in front of you in traffic, this is proof that he has a larger penis.

So let's be realistic: You still want to look good. This is not to say that you assign the same priority to mere physical appearance as to being an independent, fulfilled person. No, you assign a much *higher* priority to mere physical appearance on some occasions, such as when you're at the beach, idly pummeling your cellulite and wondering whether your varicose veins, if stretched end to end, would reach Japan, and suddenly you notice that your husband, who has been pretending to read page 13,462 of James Michener's recent blockbuster epic novel *Cleveland,* is in fact ogling a 19-year-old Barbie-shaped woman wearing a bathing suit the size of a hospital identification bracelet.

In situations like this it's quite natural for you to feel insecure, to wonder if your husband secretly wishes that *you* had the body of a 19-year-old. Trust me, this is not the case: He secretly wishes you had the body of a *16-year-old.* The slimeball. I mean, exactly how does he think you got your current set of hips? You got them from *bearing his children,* that's how. You got them from undergoing pregnancies that lasted, according to your calculations, for as long as six years apiece, during which you were forced to bloat up like Rhonda Rhinoceros through no fault of your own because your body was seized by irresistible eons-old hormonal instincts that compelled you to stop at the Dunkin' Donuts so often that they finally gave you a reserved parking space, and all so that *your husband's unborn children* would be supplied with their necessary daily nutritional input of Bavarian cream.

And, okay, even since the birth of your children, you have, on occasion, been guilty of snacking. Why? Because you were *stuck in the damned kitchen,* that's why. Because all of the grand claims your husband made, back when you were dating, about how you two were going to be Equal Housework Partners, turned out to mean in actual practice that he occasionally, with great fanfare, refills the ice-cube tray. In fourteen years of marriage he has prepared approximately four meals, at least three of which involved peanut butter, the result being that you have spent thousands of hours preparing food for the family, a job that requires you, for strictly altruistic reasons, to taste the soup and the spaghetti sauce and, yes, sometimes as much as three-quarters of the uncooked chocolate-chip-cookie dough.

And so now here you are, at the beach, stuck in a body that looks somehow alien to you, a body that seems so large that you're afraid to go swimming for fear that the Coast Guard will attempt to board you, and this is at least partly the fault of your husband, who promised to stick by you in thickness as well as health and who has not maintained his *own* body in exactly Olympic-diver condition, and the son of a bitch has the *nerve* to sit *right next* to you and stare at this *bimbo* so hard that his eyeballs have actually left their sockets and are crawling, crablike, across the sand.

Not that you are bitter.

Oh, sure, the women's magazines keep saying that it's no longer important to look young, that maturity is "in." But they never use normal mature women to illustrate this point. They use women such as Sophia Loren, an obvious genetic mutation who will continue to have the skin of a child long after the Earth has crashed into the sun. Or they use Jane Fonda, who is so obsessed with remaining inhumanly taut by working out ninety-two hours a day that it took her more than a decade to notice that she was married to a dweeb. Or they use *Cher,* for God's sake, a woman who has had so much cosmetic surgery that, for ease of maintenance, many of her body parts are attached with Velcro.

So we have to face up to the fact that there is still a flagrant double standard, wherein porky gray men like Raymond Burr are considered physically attractive, whereas women are considered over the hill moments after they reach puberty. Of course you already know this, which is why, like most middle-aged women, you're probably determined to battle the aging process unto death and beyond if necessary. Fortunately, thanks to the selfless, caring people who make up the cosmetics industry, it is now possible for you to remain surprisingly youthful-looking for at least a little longer, with no more of a daily investment in time and money than would be required to build a working steam locomotive by hand. The key, of course, is:

PROPER SKIN CARE

Your skin's number one enemy is Mister Sun, whom we used to think of as a friend. Remember? Remember when you used to lie on the beach practically naked at high noon and shout, "Take my body, Mister Sun!" I bet you even used an aluminum-foil reflector so you could catch *extra* sun rays and aim them at your flesh while you rolled around like a frankfurter on a grill to make sure your entire body was cooked until Well Done.

Of course we now realize, thanks to advances in scientific knowledge, that you were a moron. In terms of responsible skin care, you might just as well have been scrubbing yourself with Brillo pads drenched in battery acid. Because all that time, Mister Sun was bombarding you with tiny vicious invisible rays called "ultraviolets" that are slowly heating up the Earth to the point where they may ultimately destroy all life on the planet. And what is worse, they cause *dry skin.*

Even as you read these words, scientists from many nations are working feverishly to develop some practical solution to this problem, such as launching a giant orbiting plastic squeeze tube that would squirt humongous gobs of Clinique number 74 sun block all over the planet. But for now it's up to you, the individual aging woman, to deal with the problem yourself.

Step One is never go out in the daylight. Your role model here is the vampire community, whose members keep their skin attractively smooth and waxy for thousands of years. I am not suggesting here that you should live in some dank castle, sleeping in a coffin by day and venturing forth at night to drink human blood; top dermatologists agree that there's no reason why you can't keep your coffin in your current home. The important thing is that you *stay out of the sun.* You shouldn't even look at the sun on *television,* or stand in a room with bright wallpaper, or hum "Here Comes the Sun," unless you're wearing a layer of UV-blocking cream thick enough to conceal a set of car keys in.

But even if you take these precautions, your skin is eventually going to deteriorate. When you're young, your skin contains many natural fluids that make it smooth and supple, but as you age, Mother Nature, who is, let's face it, a heartless bitch, takes these fluids away from you and gives them to undeserving teenagers. This means that unless you wish to wind up with skin so dry and pebbly that the mere sight of you causes lizards to become sexually aroused, you will need to purchase vast amounts of good-quality cosmetic skin-care products. And when I say "good quality," I of course mean "costing more per one-ounce tube than a semester at Yale." You will need products designed specifically for each sector of your face, including forehead, chin, cheeks, upper lip, lower lip, left eye, right eye, upper nose, middle nose, sub-nostril zone, and wattles.

Cosmetic-industry scientists tell us that, within our lifetimes, there will be a separate skin-care product for *each individual pore,* so that you'll need to add a gymnasium-sized Skin-Care Product Storage Facility to your home, and in order to be ready to leave for work at eight A.M. you'll have to start working on your face by six P.M. the previous day. And even *that* may not be enough to keep your skin moist. You may also want to undergo a recently developed surgical procedure wherein doctors implant a miniature sprinkler system—patterned after the ones used for lawns—right in your face, with tiny sensors that cause it to spray water on your skin when they detect dryness. Of course there are still some wrinkles to be ironed out of this system, as was shown in a recent tragedy wherein a facial sprinkler installed in Mrs. Phyllis Schlafly was triggered by a restaurant candle and, before it could be brought under control, spewed out more than seventeen gallons of water, thus destroying a salad valued at nearly forty dollars. But such is the price of progress.

WEIGHT CONTROL

Have you noticed that some women just don't seem to gain weight, no matter what they eat? You'll be in a restaurant, eating a Diet Plate consisting of four tunafish molecules garnished with low-sodium parsley, and you can nevertheless actually *feel* yourself gaining weight. Meanwhile at the next table is a woman wearing a size zero dress, wolfing down a chocolate cake that had to be delivered to her table via forklift. How does she get away with it? Where does she put the calories?

The answer is: *into your body.* Yes! If you look into her purse, you'll find that she, like many modern weight-conscious women, is carrying an electronic device called a Calorie Transmaterializer, which transforms the food entering her body into invisible rays and shoots them into the body of whoever is sitting nearby. If you are so unfortunate as to be sitting near *several* hungry women with Calorie Transmaterializers, you could easily explode before they get past their appetizers. If I were you, I'd get one of these handy devices *soon.*

THE
MIDLIFE
(YAWN)
MARRIAGE

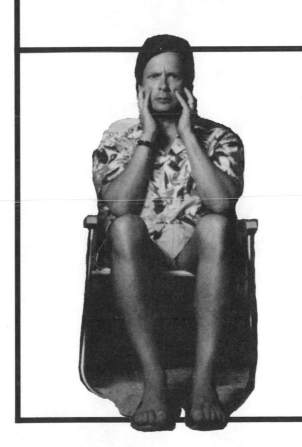

I believe it was Shake-
speare, or possibly
Howard Cosell, who first observed that marriage is very
much like a birthday candle, in that "the flames of passion burn brightest when the wick of intimacy is first
ignited by the disposable butane lighter of physical at-
traction, but sooner or later the heat of familiarity causes
the wax of boredom to drip all over the vanilla frosting
of novelty and the shredded coconut of romance."

I could not have phrased it better myself. There can be
no doubt that the institution of marriage is in serious
trouble in our society, to the point where we have to
wonder whether it can even survive. Take a look at these
alarming statistics:

- In the past decade, at least five U.S. military
  personnel have been killed by toppling vending
  machines onto themselves.
- The female pinworm lays an average of *11,000*
  eggs.

And I'm sure we would be even more alarmed if we
had some way of knowing the percentage of marriages

that end in divorce. I bet it's very high, because you rarely see couples who have been married for a long time. Nowadays, when two people manage to reach their fiftieth wedding anniversary, it's considered a news event at least as important as the U.S. trade deficit. You'll see newspaper stories with charming photographs of the couple holding hands, and heartwarming quotes about how, after all those years, they still by gosh have the hots for each other. How do they do it? What's their "secret recipe" for keeping the romance and spontaneity in their relationship after all those decades?

The answer is: senility. These people barely recognize each other. Every morning they wake up and look at each other, and they think, "Who the heck is *this?*" Novelty, that's what they have going for them. A feeling of "something different." Oh sure, you run a certain risk when you reach this level of obliviousness. If you attempt to go to the post office, there's always a chance that you'll wander off and wind up in Brazil. But that's a small price to pay for lasting romance.

Chances are, however, that you're all *too* familiar with your spouse. Chances are you feel as though you've been involved with this person since at least the Paleolithic period. You're so familiar with each other's thought processes that your "conversations" make you sound as though your brains have been surgically replaced by Random Phrase Generators:

YOU: I was thinking we . . .
YOUR SPOUSE: No, because of the . . .
YOU: Oh, right, the . . .

YOUR SPOUSE: From Cleveland.
YOU: With the, with the . . .
YOUR SPOUSE: Pit bull because of the . . .
YOU: Trash compactor.
YOUR SPOUSE: Right.

After a decade or so of marriage, you know *everything* about your spouse, every habit and opinion and twitch and tic and minor skin growth. You could write a seventeen-pound book solely about the way your spouse *eats*. This kind of intimate knowledge can be very handy in certain situations—such as when you're on a TV quiz show where the object is to identify your spouse from the sound of his or her chewing—but it tends to lower the passion level of a relationship.

Imagine, for example, a man and a woman who have been married for a dozen years. And imagine that the woman feels that their relationship has perhaps gone just a bit stale, as evidenced by the fact that since 1984 their most intimate moment together was the warm embrace they shared when they found out that their homeowners' insurance covered the unexplained explosion in their septic tank.

So let's say that one day the woman decides she is going to by God inject a spark of renewed passion into the marriage, so on her lunch hour she goes to the Frederick's of Hollywood at the mall and purchases an explicit lingerie outfit so sheer that you could read an appliance warranty through it in an unlit closet. And that night, after the children have been tucked into bed, she puts it on, and when her husband comes into the bedroom, all ready to indulge in his usual highly sensuous nighttime routine of watching the news while flossing his teeth, she is waiting for him, wearing nothing but her sexy new outfit and a sultry expression.

As he gazes upon her, standing there in her most provocative pose, he feels a sudden, unexpected stirring of excitement, stemming from the realization that *she has charged this outfit on their Visa card.* Yes, he can even see the charge slip lying on the dresser. Forty-seven dollars! My God! Here they are already *very* close to their credit limit, thanks to her incomprehensible (to him) decision to buy a brand-new clothes dryer despite the fact that he was perfectly capable of fixing the old one—he had told her this *at least* a hundred times—and now here she has spent *forty-seven dollars* on a garment that is approximately the size of a sandwich bag. This is what he is thinking as he gazes upon her, and she can tell immediately that he is not overwhelmed with lust because he is scratching himself absentmindedly in the groin region, a habit that just drives her *crazy* sometimes, especially when he has promised that he was going to do something useful, such as fix the damn clothes dryer, and instead he spends the day sprawled on the Barcalounger, watching some idiotic televised golf match and rooting around in his underwear with both hands as though he thought the Hope diamond was concealed down there.

But she is *determined* that they're going to have a romantic interlude, and so, licking her lips lasciviously, she steps toward him; and he, finally realizing—sensitive human that he is—that this would not be the ideal moment to raise the topic of household finances, steps toward her; and they draw each other close; and as their lips meet, a new feeling comes over both of them, an urgent, insistent feeling; and it is of course the feeling of their seven-year-old daughter tugging on them to inform them that their five-year-old son is throwing up on the dog.

So we can see that it is not easy to maintain a high Romance Quotient in a relationship over long periods of time. Even Romeo, if he had spent enough time under the balcony gazing up worshipfully at Juliet, would eventually have noticed her protruding nostril hairs.

The question is, what can you do about this? By "this," of course, I mean "protruding nostril hairs." Tweezers are *not* the solution, take it from me. Another important question is: How can you keep your marriage from going stale? Fortunately, there are some effective techniques you can use—reliable, time-tested techniques that I will discuss in detail just as soon as I think them up. While I'm doing that, it would be a good idea for you to take the following:

SCIENTIFIC QUIZ FOR DETERMINING HOW BAD YOUR MARRIAGE IS

1. What do you and your spouse have in common?
   a. We have essentially the same moral values, political views, and aesthetic judgments.
   b. We both like Chinese food.
   c. We are both protein-based life-forms.

2. You are most likely to share your true feelings with your spouse when you are feeling:
   a. Love.
   b. Anger.
   c. Sodium pentathol.
3. When you have a serious conversation with your spouse, the topic is most likely to be:
   a. Your relationship, and how you can make it better.
   b. Your children, and how you should rear them.
   c. Your remote control, and who gets to hold it.
4. In the special, most secret, most private moments that you and your spouse share together, you call each other:
   a. "Darling."
   b. "Lust Machine."
   c. Long distance.
5. When you and your spouse disagree, you generally try to resolve your differences via:
   a. Discussion.
   b. Argument.
   c. Assault rifle.
6. How would you describe your sex life?
   a. Fantastic.
   b. Excellent.
   c. Superb.
7. No, I mean your sex life with *each other.*
   a. Oh.
   b. Our *what?*
   c. With *each other?*
8. Men: What did you buy your wife on her last birthday?

a. Nice jewelry.
b. A new coffeemaker.
c. Bait.
9. Women: What do you usually wear to bed?
   a. A silky negligée, makeup, and several strategic dabs of Calvin Klein's "Night Moan" cologne.
   b. A cotton nightgown, a hair net, and a small yet distinctive chin smear of Crest "Tartar Control" toothpaste.
   c. A nightgown made of tent-grade flannel; a pair of official National Hockey League Wayne Gretzky Model knee socks, a sufficient number of hair curlers (in the ever-popular, highly seductive Bazooka Bubble Gum Pink) to meet the plastic needs of Western Europe for a decade; and of course "skin moisturizer" that has the same erotic appeal as industrial pump lubricant and has been applied to your face thickly enough to trap small woodland creatures.
10. If you could change just one thing about your spouse, that thing would be his or her:
   a. Tendency to snore.
   b. Physical appearance.
   c. Identity.

How to Score The correct scoring procedure is to give yourself a certain number of points for each answer, although quite frankly I think that a person in your particular marital situation ought to spend less time fooling around with some idiot quiz and more time lining up a good attorney. Or, if you're a real dreamer, you could always try:

PUTTING THE "SPARK" BACK INTO
YOUR MARRIAGE

Your best bet here is to leave the kids with your parents
and take a second honeymoon, although under no circumstances should the man (see chapter 2, "Your Disin-
tegrating Body") attempt to carry the woman across the
threshold unless your idea of an intimate evening in-
volves paramedics. But other than that, a second honeymoon is a terrific idea—a chance for the two of you to
spend some time alone, away from the numbing grind of
your daily domestic routine, with nothing to distract you
from days of pleasure and nights of passion except possibly the phone call from your mother asking if there is a
particular pediatric surgeon you generally go to, or
should she just pick one on her own. Which brings us
to our next chapter, on children as a leading cause of
old age.

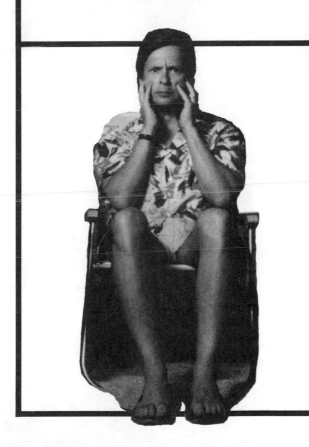

5

THE
(RAPIDLY)
AGING
PARENT

If you're like most members of the Baby Boom generation, you decided somewhere along the line, probably after about four margaritas, to have children. This was inevitable. Mother Nature, in her infinite wisdom, has instilled within each of us a powerful biological instinct to reproduce; this is her way of assuring that the human race, come what may, will never have any disposable income.

Of course, there's more to parenthood than mere biology. Parenthood is also an opportunity for each of us to advance the cause of civilization by passing along to the next generation—as our parents passed along to us—the cherished values and ideals, developed over thousands of years, that define what the human race truly stands for, namely:

- "Don't spit."
- "How do you *know* you hate asparagus when you haven't even *tried* it?"
- "No, you are NOT going to get a snake."
- "I said DON'T SPIT!"

- "Well, how do *you* suppose your underpants got into the microwave? Do you suppose they just crawled in there *by themselves?*"
- "All right then, but it's going to be YOUR snake, and I expect YOU to take care of it."
- "If you spit on your sister ONE MORE TIME, there is going to be NO MORE TELEVISION until THANKSGIVING and I MEAN IT!!"
- "Yes I KNOW Daddy called Mr. Stimson a dickhead, but that does NOT mean that YOU may call Mr. Stimson a dickhead."
- "NO, YOU ARE *NOT* GOING TO GET A DOG, NOT AFTER WHAT HAPPENED TO THE SNAKE."

And so on. Yes, parenthood can be difficult, but it also has its rewards. In the end, there's no substitute for the sense of satisfaction that comes from watching as your children, under your steady guiding hand, develop from tiny, helpless Frequent Barfer modules into full-grown, self-reliant young adults fully capable of crashing your car into a day-care center.

Of course, we must remember that growth is not a "one-way street." As our children grow, so must we grow to meet their changing emotional, intellectual, and designer-footwear needs. In this chapter we'll examine some of the challenges that we face as parental units entering middle age, a time when we are coming to the somber realization that we will not always be there to guide and direct our children, which is just as well, because this is also a time when our children are coming to the conclusion that we are unbelievable dorks.

One big reason for this, of course, is our taste in music. I'm assuming that you're like most of us Boomers in the sense that, musically, you have always considered yourself to be a Major Hipster. Why not? Hey, we were front-line troops in the Rock 'n' Roll Revolution, right? Damn straight! We were Born to Boogie. We grew up dancing the Twist, the Mashed Potato, the Boogaloo, the Jerk, the Watusi, the Pony, the Alligator, the Clam, and the Vicious Bloodsucking Insect. We knew the dirty words to "Louie Louie," including the ones that did not actually exist. We knew the Beach Boys when they could sing and Elvis when he was alive the *first* time. We knew the Beatles and the Stones when they were actual bands as opposed to multinational corporations. We were *there* during the legendary sixties, with visions and insights and lava lamps and black lights and sitar music and really *dynamite* home-grown weed that would get you high in only 178 tokes. We lit candles and sat around listening to John Lennon sing, with genuine passion in his voice, about how he was the egg man, and *they* were the egg men, and *he* was also the walrus, and by God we knew *exactly what he meant.* That was the level of hipness that we attained, in My Generation. Oh sure, people tried to put us down, just because we got around. Our parents would come into our bedroom, where we were listening to the opening guitar lick of "Purple Haze" with the stereo cranked up loud enough to be audible on Mars (which is where Jimi Hendrix originated) and they'd hold their hands over their ears and make a face as though they were passing a kidney stone the size of a volleyball and they'd shout: "You call that *music?* That sounds like somebody strangling a *cat.*" Our parents' idea of swinging music was Frank Sinatra snapping his fingers in front of sixty-seven guys who looked like your dentist playing the trombone. Our parents danced *holding hands,* for God's sake. They did the "fox trot," which was invented by the Phoenicians. They were totally Out Of It, our parents. Hopeless. They were so square they thought that people, other than Maynard G. Krebs, actually *used* words like "square." As Bob Dylan, who was so hip that sometimes even *he* didn't understand what he meant, put it: "Something is happening here, and you don't know what it is, do you, Mr. Jones?" That was our parents: Mr. and Mrs. Jones. But not us. We *defined* hip. We set all kinds of world hipness records, and we were sure they'd never be broken.

Then came the seventies, and the major new musical trends were (1) disco, which consisted of one single song approximately 14,000 minutes long; and (2) heavy metal, which consisted of skinny, hostile, pockmarked men wearing outfits that looked as though they had smeared toxic waste on their bodies, playing what sounded like amplified jackhammers and shrieking unintelligibly at auditoriums full of whooping, sweating, hyperactive, boot-wearing, tattooed people who indicated their approval by giving each other head injuries with chairs. We old-time rock 'n' rollers looked at this scene, and we said, "Nah." We were sure it would pass. So we played our Buffalo Springfield albums and our Motown dance tapes, and we waited for the day when good music, *hip* music, would become popular again.

By the eighties, a lot of radio stations, realizing the size of the market out there, had started playing sixties music again. They called it "classic rock," because they knew we'd be upset if they came right out and called it what it is, namely "middle-aged-person nostalgia music." It's a very popular format now. You drive through a major urban area and push the "scan" button on your car radio, and you'll probably hear a dozen "classic rock" stations, ten of which will be playing "Doo-wah diddy diddy." (The other two will be playing *commercials* featuring "Doo-wah diddy diddy.") We hear "classic rock" being played constantly in elevators, department stores, offices, churches, operating rooms, the space shuttle, etc. Almost every sixties group with at least one remaining non-dead member has reunited and bought new dentures and gone on tour, sometimes using special guitars equipped with walkers.

And so, because we represent the world's largest consumer horde, we get to hear Our Music all the time. We're wrapped in a snug, warm cocoon of sixtiesness, and we actually think that we're still With It. Whereas in fact we are nowhere near It. The light leaving from It right now will not reach us for several years. I've become intensely aware of this through my son, who, despite constant exposure to my taste in music, does NOT choose to listen to "classic rock." When he's in control of the radio, he tunes it to a different kind of music, a new kind of music, a *now* kind of music that can only be described—and I do not mean to be making any value judgments here—as "stupid."

If you have kids, you probably know the music I mean.

It sounds as though an evil scientist had gone into his laboratory and, for some insane reason, *combined disco with heavy metal.* It has no melody and hardly any words; it consists almost entirely of bass notes registering 7.4 on the Richter scale. It's music to slaughter cattle by. It's the kind of music you hear emanating from refrigerator-sized boom boxes and black 1974 Camaros that have windows tinted so dark you could safely view a solar eclipse through them and sound systems so powerful that with every beat the sides of the car actually bulge outward, like in a Warner Brothers cartoon, such that you can't imagine how any form of life could survive in there. If you're unfamiliar with this kind of music, hold this page right up close to your ear for a second and I'll play a sample for you:

BOOM boom BOOM boom BOOM boom BOOM!
BOOM boom BOOM boom BOOM boom BOOM!
BOOM boom BOOM boom BOOM boom BOOM!
BOOM boom BOOM boom BOOM boom BOOM!
(repeat chorus)

Isn't that *awful?* That's what my son likes to listen to. This leads to conflict when we're in the car. He'll push the radio button for BOOM boom BOOM etc., and then I, in a loving parental effort to guide him toward a more sophisticated and meaningful cultural experience, will thoughtfully swat his hand aside and push the button for Doo-wah diddy diddy. Then he'll lean back in his seat and look at me with exactly the same disgusted look that I aimed at my parents thirty years ago when they made me take my Buddy Holly 45s off of our RCA phonograph so they could play Rosemary Clooney.

And I think: Something is happening here, and I don't know what it is. And neither does Bob Dylan.

Another area in which my son makes me feel old is fashion. Especially hair fashion. I've always considered myself to be extremely liberal when it came to hair, because I remember how much I hated the hair hassles I went through back in the sixties when I had long hair. I'd be walking past a clot of geezers who were sitting in front of a volunteer fire department, hoping somebody's house would catch fire so they could watch the trucks pull out, and one of them would invariably look at me and say, in a tone of voice suggesting that this was the cleverest and most original remark ever thought up by anybody with the possible exception of Mark Twain, "Hey, is that a BOY or a GIRL??" This awesome display of wit never failed to absolutely slay the other geezers, who'd laugh themselves into various stages of coronary seizure ("har har har har hack hack hack hack hawk hawk HAWK SPIT"), and I, being a Flower Child Peace Person in the Summer of Love, would give them the finger. But I would also vow to myself that no matter how old I got, I would never, ever, hassle anybody about his haircut.

Of course, back then there was no such thing as "punk."

So anyway, for the first few years after my son was born, things were fairly frictionless on the haircut front. My son favored the Dwight Eisenhower style so popular with babies, consisting of approximately eight wisps of hair occasionally festooned with creamed spinach. When he grew real hair, I'd take him to the barbershop and request that he be given a regular haircut, defined as "a haircut exactly like mine."

Then one day, when he was six, he came home from school, which is where they pick this stuff up, and announced that he wanted a punk haircut. Remembering my experiences in the sixties, I sat him down and thoughtfully explained to him that although I, personally, did not care for the punk style of haircut, the real issue here was personal freedom of choice, and since it was, after all, his hair, then by gosh if he really, really wanted to, he could get a punk haircut just as soon as I had been dead and buried for a minimum of forty-five years.

I thought that this honest sharing of feelings had settled the matter, so you can imagine my surprise when, about a week later, my son went to the mall with my wife, whom I will never fully trust again, and came home looking like Sid Vicious. His hair was very short around the sides except for a little tail going down the back of his neck, as though the barber had suddenly remembered an important appointment and had to rush off without finishing my son. The hair on the top was smeared with what appeared to be transmission fluid and sticking up in spikes, which made it look like a marine creature striking a defensive posture.

I really, really hate this haircut, and, needless to say, my son really, really loves it. He is constantly checking himself out in the mirror and performing routine spike maintenance. I'll say: "It's time for your bedtime story!"

And he'll say: "Not now! I'm gelling my hair!"

And of course it's just going to get worse. I'm constantly being assured of this by the parents of teenagers. "You think his *haircut* is bad?" they say. "Wait until he wants an earring." Which of course he will. In fact he'll probably want an earring in his *nose,* as part of his ongoing, totally instinctive campaign to make me feel like a fossilized fud.

I'll tell you what would *really* age me fast: if I had a teenaged daughter. I don't think I could handle that. Because that would mean that teenaged boys would be coming around to my house. "Hi, Mr. Barry!" they'd say, with their cheerful, innocent young voices. "We're here to have sex with your daughter!"

No, of course they wouldn't come out and *say* that, but I know that's what they'd be *thinking,* because I was a teenaged boy once, and I was basically a walking hormone storm. I'm sure modern boys are no different. So if I had a teenaged daughter, and a boy came to my house, after somehow picking his way through the land mines in the lawn, I'd probably lunge through the screen door and strangle him right there ("Hi, Mr. Barry! Is Jennifer heAAAAAAAWWWWK").

You think I'm exaggerating, but I have male friends whose daughters are approaching puberty at speeds upwards of 700 miles per hour, and when you say the word "dating," my friends get a look in their eyes that makes Charles Manson look like Captain Kangaroo. So in some ways I'm relieved that I don't have daughters, although in other ways I envy people with daughters, because little girls tend to be thoughtful, whereas little boys tend to be—and I say this as a loving father who would not trade his son for anything in the world—jerks.

I used to think this was society's fault. This was back in the idealistic sixties and seventies, when we Boomers had many excellent child-rearing theories and no actual children. Remember those days? Remember when we truly believed that if society treated boys and girls exactly the same, then they wouldn't be bound by sexual stereotypes, and the boys could grow up to be sensitive and the girls could grow up to be linebackers? Ha ha! Boy, were we ever idealistic! By which I mean "stupid." Because when we look at actual children, no matter how they are raised, we notice immediately that little girls are in fact smaller versions of real human beings, whereas little boys are Pod People from the Planet Destructo. I don't think society has anything to do with this. I think that if you had two desert islands, and you put girl babies on one island and boy babies on another island, and they somehow were able to survive with no help from adult society, eventually the girls would cooperate in collecting pieces of driftwood and using them to build shelters, whereas the boys would pretend that driftwood pieces were guns. (Yes, I realize they'd have no way of knowing what guns were. This would not stop them.) Not only that, but even if the island had 176,000 pieces of driftwood on it, the boys would all end up violently arguing over *one* of them.

I base my opinions on several years of working in an office located in a house with a large transient little-boy population. Individually they're okay, but if two of them get together, their combined total IQ is immediately halved, and if a third boy comes along it's halved *again*, and so on, so that if you have, say, six of them, you're talking about the destructive force of a tank commanded by the brainpower of a Labrador retriever. They communicate with each other by slamming doors. They have the attention span of gnats. "STOP SLAMMING THE DOORS!" I'll yell at them. "Okay!" they'll reply (SLAM). They are so busy running around and arguing and breaking things and strewing random objects over every square inch of floor that they barely have time to pee, and they *definitely* don't have time to aim. They just race into the bathroom, let loose in any old random direction, and then race out again, because by God there are doors to be slammed.

Not that I'm complaining. For reasons I can't explain, I really like being a parent. It's just that there's a lot more *to* it than I expected. Take school projects. A school project is a kind of activity designed by educators to provide our children with valuable learning experiences that they would carry with them for the rest of their lives if they were capable of remembering anything for longer than three-tenths of a second, which unfortunately they are not. At least my son isn't. If I want to make sure he has his shoes on by Monday morning, I have to start reminding him no later than Saturday afternoon.

"Robert," I'll say, while he is engaged in some vital activity such as pouring PurpleSaurus Rex flavor Kool-Aid on the patio to form a Liquefied Sugar Theme Park for ants, "I want you to put on your shoes *right now.*"

"Okay," he'll say, with total sincerity. Meanwhile, inside his skull, a small but powerful organ found in children and known to medical science as the Instruction Diverter has taken my words as they entered his left ear and, before they could begin to penetrate his brain, ejected them out his right ear at nearly the speed of light. He continues to stare at the ants.

"What did I just ask you?" I'll ask.

"What?" he'll answer. He has *no idea* what we're talking about. At that very moment my instructions are whizzing past the asteroid belt.

"I WANT YOU TO PUT YOUR SHOES ON RIGHT NOW!" I'll say.

"Okay!" he'll say, irritated that I'm yelling at him for absolutely no reason. If I squint, I can actually see my words shooting out his ear as he continues to stare at the ants, who are scurrying around putting on tiny ant shoes because even *they* have a better ability to retain instructions than Robert.

Of course, my son is perfectly normal. (Right? RIGHT??) A lot of children have trouble remembering instructions, which is why we parents often find out about school projects at the very last minute, usually from other parents. "Didn't you hear?" they'll say. "Each child is supposed to come in tomorrow with a model medieval village made entirely from typewriter parts."

School projects generally contain an element of inexplicable weirdness. I think this is a form of revenge on the part of the teachers, getting even with us parents for spending our day in adult company while they're stuck in crowded rooms trying to get our children to stop writing their 5's backward. I bet they have fun at teachers' meetings, thinking up projects to inflict on us. ("I've got it! We have them make a cement volcano that erupts real ketchup!" "No, we had them do that last year.")

Whatever they come up with, we do it, because we want our children to succeed in school so they'll eventually graduate and we won't have to do projects anymore. Science Fair projects are the worst. Parents go completely insane at Science Fair time, which is why you see second-graders showing up with small fusion reactors that they allegedly made themselves. I know a woman named Janice who became so deranged by an approaching Science Fair that she actually spat in her daughters' Knox unflavored gelatin. I'm not making this up. Her two daughters were doing projects that were supposed to demonstrate how common household molds would grow in little containers of gelatin, and so naturally the mold refused to grow. Isn't that just like mold? When you DON'T want it to grow, such as when company is coming, it flourishes, especially around the base of the toilet. Whereas when you really WANT it to grow, when you have gone to the supermarket and purchased FOOD for it, it does nothing. Mold is scum.

So anyway, the Science Fair was approaching, and Janice's daughters were getting more and more upset, and finally, late one night when they were asleep, Janice spat in their gelatin. The mold grew like crazy, thereby demonstrating the important scientific principle that school projects can cause normal adults to lose all contact with reality.

This is why one year, the night before my son's project was due, my wife and I got into an emotional kitchen argument over buoyancy. Buoyancy had never before played much of a role in our relationship, but it was the subject of Robert's project, and he and I had spent the afternoon driving frantically from store to store trying to locate the items we needed, including cork and plastic bottles and a special kind of foam board that your child absolutely HAS to have for his project backdrop or you will be arrested for child abuse.

So by nightfall I was *heavily* involved in buoyancy, and you can imagine how I felt when my wife looked at the project—which showed scientifically how come corks float and rocks sink—and she said she didn't understand it. She said she thought corks floated because they were light and rocks sank because they were heavy. This is also what I always thought, but I wasn't about to admit it, not after the work I'd put into this project. So I told her that she was crazy, and that anybody who knows anything about science knows that corks float because of buoyancy, which is related to displacement, which is caused by plastic bottles. I admit I was bluffing, but I was damned if I was going to let anybody attack my Science Fair project. Robert, meanwhile, had wandered off. Children have too much sense to become overly involved in their educations.

What scares me most about parenting is that I'm really just starting out. There are plenty of scary parts that I haven't even gotten to yet. Driving, for example. In most states you can get a driver's license when you're 16 years old, which made a lot of sense to me when I was 16 years old but now seems insane. I mean, my son is 9, which means that most states consider him to be more than halfway old enough to drive, and we are talking about a person who still sleeps on *Return of the Jedi* sheets. So I am definitely in favor of raising the minimum driving age. In fact, I think it should be raised every year, to keep my son from ever reaching it. I think that when my son is 58 years old and comes to visit me in the Old Persons' Home, he should arrive via skateboard.

And then there are the money worries. You need a lot of money to raise a modern child. Hair gel alone will run you thousands of dollars. And let's not forget Mr. Orthodontist, with his private jet and his villa in Switzerland. He is sure to notice that your child's teeth have come in backwards, or some other terrible problem that can only be corrected via an orthodontic project comparable in scope to the interstate highway system, only more expensive. This will of course prevent you from saving any money to put your child through college, which, as you know from reading numerous alarming articles, will be so expensive by the time your child is old enough that the only way you'll be able to afford it will be by selling your body parts—a kidney for freshman year, a section of liver for sophomore year, maybe an eyeball for that all-important junior year abroad, etc. God help you if your children decide to go to graduate school. You'll wind up being carried to the commencement exercises in a cigar box.

But it will be worth the sacrifice, knowing that you've done all you can to prepare your children to go out and make their way, on their own, in the Real World. Although they'll probably decide it's easier to just move back in with you.

PLANNING
YOUR
MALE
MIDLIFE
CRISIS

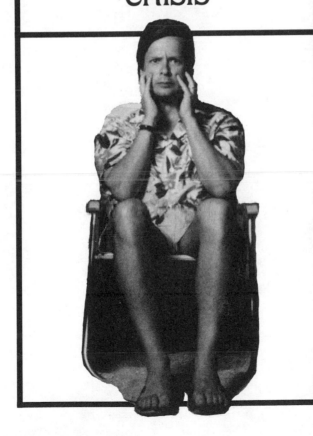

The past twenty years have seen tremendous advances in our understanding of these mysterious creatures called men—what motivates them; what kinds of complex and subtle emotions they're really experiencing underneath their brusque "macho" exteriors; and why they are all basically slime-sucking toads. Most of this understanding has been supplied by popular psychologists, dedicated men and women who—despite the very real risk that they will have to appear on the Oprah Winfrey Show—are constantly churning out insightful groundbreaking books with titles like:

- Men Who Hate Women
- Men Who Claim Not to Hate Women But Trust Me They Are Lying
- Men Who Okay, Maybe They Don't Hate ALL Women, But They Definitely Cannot Stand YOU

And so on. Reading between the lines, we can see that men do not have a terrific reputation for being dependable, lifelong partners in a relationship. In this chapter we will put on our pith helmets and begin to explore a major reason for this—namely, the midlife crisis. This is a phase that all men are required, by federal law, to go through, as part of the Official Popular-Psychology Schedule of:

MALE LIFESTYLE PHASES

AGE	PHASE	INTERESTS
0–2	Infancy	Pooping
3–9	Innocence	Guns
10–13	Awareness	Sex
14–20	Emancipation	Sex
21–29	Empowerment	Sex
30–39	Attainment	Sex
40–65	MIDLIFE CRISIS OCCURS HERE	
66–Death	Contemplation	Pooping

We can see from this scientific chart that if you're a male who has reached age 40, you should be preparing for this exciting lifestyle phase.

WHAT IS A MALE MIDLIFE CRISIS?

Basically, it's when a man, reaching his middle years, takes stock of his life and decides that *it isn't enough*—that although he has a loving wife, nice kids, a decent job, and many caring friends, he feels that he is trapped—that there is still *something more he must do,* something that we will call, for want of a better term, "making a fool of himself."

The first thing you have to understand is that this is perfectly natural. The midlife crisis occurs in virtually all males, including members of the animal kingdom. A good example is the caterpillar. He will spend a large part of his life on a predictable career path, engaging in traditional caterpillar activities such as crawling around and munching on the leaves of expensive ornamental shrubbery, and then one day, out of the blue, he'll say to his wife, "Dammit, Louise, I'm *sick* of shrubbery." She does not understand him, of course. Partly this is because she has a brain the size of an electron, but mostly it is because he seems like a complete stranger to her, a different insect altogether. Soon he has left her to live in his own cocoon, from which he eventually emerges with a whole new youthful "look"—wings, bright colors, gold jewelry, etc. As he soars into the sky, feeling fulfilled and exhilarated, free at last from the restrictive routines of his humdrum former life, Louise watches him from far below. She feels conflicting emotions: sorrow, for she knows that she has lost her mate forever; but also a strange kind of joy, for she also knows, as she watches his multihued wings flashing in the glorious golden-red glow of the sinking sun, that he is about to be eaten by a bat.

Fortunately, this rarely happens to human males. Unfortunately, what happens to human males is worse. There is virtually no end to the humiliating activities (see chapter 2, on "hair transplants") that a man will engage in while in the throes of a midlife crisis. He will destroy a successful practice as a certified public accountant to pursue a career in Roller Derby. He will start wearing enormous pleated pants and designer fragrances ("Ralph Lauren's Musque de Stud Hombre: For the Man Who Wants a Woman Who Wants a Man Who Smells Vaguely Like a Horse"). He will encase his pale, porky body in tank tops and a "pouch"-style swimsuit the size of a gum wrapper. He will buy a boat shaped like a marital aid. He will abandon his attractive and intelligent wife to live with a 19-year-old aerobics instructor who once spent an *entire summer* reading a single *Glamour* magazine article entitled "Ten Tips for Terrific Toenails."

And if this is a particularly severe case of the male midlife crisis, if this male has has no idea whatsoever how pathetic he looks, if he has lost all touch with reality, he will run for President of the United States. This is why every fourth year, just before the caucuses, Iowa becomes positively infested with obscure, uninspiring, middle-aged political figures, racing around the state with an air of great urgency and self-importance, issuing "position papers," lunging out of shadows to shake the hands of startled Iowans, demonstrating their concern for agriculture by frowning thoughtfully at pigs, etc. You see this on the evening news, and your reaction, as an informed voter, is: "What is *possessing* these dorks?" I mean, it is not as though they are responding to some massive groundswell of popular support. It is not as though large crowds of voters showed up at their homes and shrieked, "Hey, Congressperson! Please go to Iowa and reveal the key elements of your four-point tax-incentive plan for revitalizing heavy industry!" No, these tragically misguided men are acting on their own, trying to deny their own humdrum mediocrity, seeking desperately to inject some drama into their lives, and we could view the whole thing as harmless entertainment were it not for the fact that one of them invariably winds up becoming the leader of the Free World.

I'm going to assume that you're not a member of Congress, and that you therefore have a certain minimum amount of dignity. Nevertheless, you will eventually experience a midlife crisis, and if you're not careful, it could destroy everything you've worked so hard to build over the years. This is why it is so important that you recognize the problems that arise during this critical phase, and develop a practical, thoughtful strategy for dealing with them. This chapter will not help at all.

WHAT TRIGGERS THE MIDLIFE CRISIS

Generally the midlife crisis is triggered when a male realizes one day at about 2:30 P.M. that he has apparently, for some reason, devoted his entire life to doing something he hates. Let's say he's a lawyer. He did not just become a lawyer overnight. He worked *hard* to become a lawyer. He made enormous sacrifices, such as drinking domestic beer, so that he could afford to go to law school. He studied for thousands of hours, sweated out the law boards, groveled to get into a firm, licked a lot of shoes to make partner, and now, finally, he has made it. And then one afternoon, while writing yet another deadly dull formal letter to a client, a letter filled with standardized, prefabricated phrases such as "please be advised" and "with reference to the aforementioned subject matter," he rereads what he has just written, and it says, "Please be advised to stick the aforementioned subject matter into your personal orifice." He may not be a trained psychologist, but he recognizes latent hostility when he sees it. And so he starts to think. And the more he thinks, the more he realizes that he hates *everything about* being a lawyer. He hates his clients. He (needless to say) hates other lawyers. He hates the way every time he tells people what he does for a living, they react as though he had said "Nazi medical researcher." He hates his office. He hates Latin phrases. He hates his *briefcase.* He hates it all, just hates it hates it hates it, and finally he decides that he really wants to have a *completely different* job, something fun, something carefree, something like . . . hang-gliding instructor. Yes! That's it! He tried hang-gliding once, on vacation, and he loved it!

Meanwhile, somewhere out there is a middle-aged hang-gliding instructor who has just discovered that he hates *his* life. He hates not making enough money to own a nice car. He hates sudden downdrafts. He hates having to be nice to vacationing lawyers. What he really wants is a better-paying job that enables him to do something truly *useful* with his life. Yes, the more he thinks about it, the more he wishes that he had become . . . a doctor.

Of course, if he did a little research, he'd find that most doctors hate the medical profession. They hate getting sued. They hate the way everybody assumes that they're rich (they *are* rich, of course; they just hate the way everybody *assumes* it). They hate their beepers. They hate peering into other people's personal orifices. They wish

they had a career with less responsibility and fewer re-
strictions, a *fun* career that permitted them to drink heavily on the job and squander entire afternoons seeing how
loud they could burp. In other words, they wish they
were: humor writers.

My point is that there's no reason for you to feel depressed about being trapped in Career Hell, because so
is everybody else. Doesn't that make you feel better? No?
Hey, look, at least *you* can put this book down and go
watch TV if you feel like it. *I* have to sit here and finish
this stupid chapter so I can meet my stupid deadline. You
think it's easy, being a humor writer? You think it's *fun,*
sitting here all day in my underwear, trying to think up
new material? *You* try it sometime! You'd hate it! Especially my underwear! You'd soon see why I've reached
the point where I'd give anything to have a job in which
I could wear a nice suit and write in standardized, prefabricated phrases. As soon as I finish the aforementioned
chapter, I'm applying to law school.

Is there any proven method for coping with a midlife
career crisis? If you put that question to a group of leading psychologists, they wouldn't bother to answer you.
They're *sick* of dealing with your pathetic little problems.
They want to be test pilots. So I'll just tell you the answer: Yes, there *is* a proven method for coping with the
male midlife crisis; a method that enables you to have the
stability and security of a conventional lifestyle PLUS an
element of adventure and excitement; a method that has
been employed for years with great success by thoughtful, sophisticated male role models such as Batman.
That's right: I'm talking about having a *secret identity.* No

doubt you have often asked yourself, "Why *does* Batman have a secret identity? Why doesn't he just come out and announce that he is Bruce Wayne, wealthy millionaire, so that the police chief could simply call him up when there was trouble, instead of shining that idiot Bat Signal into the sky? I mean, what if Bruce Wayne doesn't happen to be *looking* when the Bat Signal is turned on? What if he's in the bathroom? Or doesn't he ever *go* to the bathroom? Is that why he's always sort of grimacing? Is that why he . . ."

All RIGHT. Shut UP. The point is that Bruce Wayne doesn't need a secret identity for any crime-fighting reason; he needs it because he's supposed to be a grown man, and his wealthy millionaire friends would laugh at him if they found out that he was wearing tights and driving around in a Batmobile chasing after the Joker (who, when he's not wearing *his* secret-identity disguise, is a gynecologist).

WHAT A WOMAN CAN DO WHEN HER HUSBAND IS HAVING HIS MIDLIFE CRISIS

If your husband is exhibiting signs of a midlife crisis, at first you should try to humor him. If he wants to buy a ludicrously impractical sports car, tell him you think it's a terrific idea. If he wants to wear "younger" clothes, help him pick them out. If he wants to start seeing other women, shoot him in the head.

7

SEX
AFTER 40
(OR, *SEX*?
AFTER *40*?)

I realize that sex is a delicate subject, so please be assured that in this chapter I intend to discuss it in a mature and tasteful manner devoid of such expressions as "getting a boner." But we definitely need to take a long, hard, penetrating look at sexuality, because, as we find ourselves plunging deeper and deeper into middle age, it becomes increasingly important that we have the knowledge we need to maintain a firm intellectual grasp on our private parts, so we can avoid becoming victimized by:

COMMON MYTHS ABOUT SEX AND AGING

The biggest myth, as measured by square footage, is that as you grow older, you gradually lose your interest in sex. This myth probably got started because younger people seem to want to have sex with each other at every available opportunity including traffic lights, whereas older people are more likely to reserve their sexual activities for special occasions such as the installation of a new Pope.

But does this mean that, as an aging person, you're no longer capable of feeling the lust that you felt as an 18-year-old? Not at all! You're attracted just as strongly as you ever were toward 18-year-olds! The problem is that everybody your *own* age seems repulsive.

This is the fault of the advertising industry, which goes out of its way to make aging appear to be as attractive a process as death by maggot. When the advertising industry wants to convey the concept of glamour, it fills its commercials with beautiful young people who have Ph.D.'s in bodily tautness, writhing sensuously around the product as though it's making them so excited that at any moment they're going to have sex with each other, or possibly even the product. Whereas when you see older people in advertisements, they're usually having demeaning conversations with relentlessly cheerful pharmacists:

PHARMACIST: Hi, Mr. Hopkins! You're looking even more wretched than usual today!

OLDER PERSON: Yes, Bob, it's this darned swollen hemorrhoidal tissue.

PHARMACIST: Could you say that louder, Mr. Hopkins? I'm not sure that everybody in the entire store could hear you!

OLDER PERSON: I SAID IT'S THIS DARNED SWOLLEN HEMORRHOIDAL TISSUE.

PHARMACIST (brightening): I see!

OLDER PERSON: It feels like I'm sitting on a grapefruit.

GATHERING AUDIENCE OF INTERESTED SHOPPERS: Yuck.

PHARMACIST: Don't worry, Mr. Hopkins! Because we have a product here that . . .

OLDER PERSON: Also I have horrible arthritis pain.

PHARMACIST: Well, that's no problem either! Because this product contains an amazing new ingredient called . . .

OLDER PERSON: Also my dentures are encrusted with brownish gunk and frequently fall out in public restaurants.

VOICE FROM CROWD: Stone him!

OTHERS: Yes! Stone him!

So we see that the image of aging created by advertising is not entirely glamorous. So naturally, as we grow older, we tend to assume that we should become less active sexually. In fact, however, there is no biological reason for this assumption. This was proved in a famous experiment wherein biologists placed laboratory rats in cages and allowed them to age for several years, during which they (the biologists) made the following observations:

1. The rats displayed no interest in sex. The rats displayed an interest only in pooping and looking nervous, even when the biologists read letters aloud to them from the "Penthouse Forum."
2. The biologists, on the other hand, regularly became horny, especially during the Christmas party.

So there's no reason for us to feel that getting older should stop us from having sex. Our role model in this area should be such biblical stud muffins as Job, who, if I remember my Sunday school lessons correctly, remained sexually active for several hundred years. Of course I vaguely recall that at one point in the story, all of Job's cattle and relatives died and he got boils all over his body, which should serve as a reminder to all of us, no matter what our age, of the importance of practicing safe sex.

With that in mind, there's no reason why we can't continue to lead sexually fulfilling lives well into our Golden Years, as millions of older people have done before us—including, for all we know, your own parents. Yes! It's possible! Your parents having sex! I realize that this is difficult to accept. Most of us have trouble believing that our parents *ever* had sex, even when they conceived us. Deep down inside, we believe that our mothers got pregnant because of fallout from atomic testing during the Truman administration.

But the truth is that our parents were probably engaging in sex, and some of them still do, and we can, too. Physiologically, there is absolutely nothing to prevent us from remaining sexually active into our sixties and seventies and even eighties, except of course the possibility that Doing It will cause sudden death. This has been known to happen. In the interest of common decency I am not going to name any names, but this is apparently what happened to a billionaire who was Vice-President of the United States under Gerald Ford and whose name rhymes with "Pelson Pockefeller." He was allegedly working late one night on a book with a "research assistant," and all of a sudden, probably right in the middle of an important footnote, bang, so to speak, old Pelson was *gone*.

But this is unlikely to happen to you. For one thing,

you don't even *have* a research assistant. Nevertheless, it's important that when you engage in sex during your middle and older years, you follow the:

U.S. SURGEON GENERAL'S RECOMMENDATIONS FOR OLDER PEOPLE HAVING SEX

1. Use only low-sodium margarine.
2. No whips, chains, or appliances requiring more than 200 watts.
3. No poultry.
4. No playing "Mister Johnson Goes to the Circus."

If you bear these commonsense rules in mind, there's no reason why you can't enjoy a vigorous and satisfying sex life, unless of course you happen to be a guy, in which case there's a good chance that at some point you'll have an experience wherein your partner is all ready to have sex, and you *want* to have sex, but no matter how hard you try, you can't seem to get any crisp in your cucumber (or, if you prefer strict medical terminology, any pop in your pickle). If this happens to you more than once, you may start wondering if maybe, just possibly:

You Are Impotent!

If this happens, the important thing is not to dwell on the idea that

You Are Impotent!

Because the odds are that the whole thing is purely psychological. The odds are that your organs are just fine, but for some reason your subconscious is telling you that

You Are Impotent!

over and over and over again, like a broken record, hammering home the message that

You Are Impotent!

until finally you start to *believe* it. Psychiatrists agree that if this happens, the best thing for you to do is

You Are Impotent!

No! Shut up! Stop! Psychiatrists say the best

You Are Impotent!

I'm sorry, but it's no use. I can't finish this paragraph.

Ha ha! Just a little impotency humor there. Really, there's really no reason to worry about this, because even if it turns out that

You Really *Are* Impotent!

there are all kinds of medical things they can do to you now involving surgical implants and valves and switches and remote-control devices, so that you'll be able to get an erection not only when you wish to have sex, but also whenever anybody within a mile of you operates a microwave oven. Which may not sound so terrific, but at least we guys don't have to go through:

THE CHANGE

This is the stage that a woman goes through when her body, through a complex biological process, senses that the woman has reached the stage in her life where her furniture is much too nice for her to have a baby barfing on it. So the body stops producing estrogen, which is the hormone that causes certain distinct female characteristics such as ovulation and the ability not to watch football. This bodily change is called "menopause," from the ancient Greek words *meno* (meaning "your skin sometimes gets so hot") and *pause* (meaning "that it melts Tupperware"). Also some women tend to become emotional and easily irritated by minor things that never used to bother them, such as when their husbands leave a partly used meatloaf sandwich in bed, as though the Meatloaf Sandwich Fairy were going to come along and pick it up for him.

The traditional way to cope with menopause is to ask your physician to prescribe costly pharmaceuticals, but of course these can cause harmful side effects. The pharmaceuticals industry Code of Ethics does not allow the production of any product unless merely pronouncing its chemical name in front of laboratory rats causes at least a third of them to die. So more and more, health experts are recommending a "holistic" approach, in which you develop a deeper understanding of the natural process that your body is going through, and then, with this newfound knowledge as your guide, you stick the meatloaf sandwich into the breast pocket of your husband's best suit.

8

TIME MANAGEMENT (TIP: READ THIS CHAPTER VERY QUICKLY)

Remember when you were a kid, and it seemed as though there was too *much* time? I can remember, at around age 9, having so much spare time, especially during the summer, that I could afford to spend entire *days* on activities such as coloring my entire stomach blue with a ballpoint pen, or breaking the world's record for Highest Pile of Cheerios Stuck Together with Peanut Butter, or conducting a scientific experiment to see exactly how many candles the dog would eat before it started walking funny.

Well, those innocent days are long gone. Today, as grownups, we're all so busy rushing madly around trying to meet the demands of families, friends, careers, homes, etc., that we barely have time for personal hygiene, which many people now are forced to perform in the car. Especially women. Most women manage to arrive at work looking terrific, but a lot of them got into their cars looking like Oonga, She-Walrus of the North. Driving to work on I-95 in Miami, I have seen women styling their hair, putting on makeup, sometimes even sticking their arms out the windows on both sides of the car to be worked on by professional manicurists riding motorcycles. Of course, this requires them to take their hands off the wheel, but in Miami (Official Driving Motto: "Death Before Yielding") this actually gives them an advantage.

Male drivers, of course, generally don't engage in such automotive beauty regimens. Males like to save their precious car time for picking their noses. For some reason, males think that car windows have one-way glass, so when they stop at a red light, even with cars all around them, they'll start rooting around their nostrils as though they have a gold brick in there. This is why truly classy individuals such as Donald Trump have those dark-tinted windows on their limousines. (Not that I'm suggesting here that Donald Trump picks his nose. That's why he has a *staff,* for God's sake.)

My point is that the older you get, the less you can afford to fritter away your valuable time on wasteful and stupid activities such as reading either of the two preceding paragraphs. You need to learn some proven time-management techniques, which we'll get to after we kill a few more minutes here with:

A BRIEF AND HIGHLY INACCURATE HISTORY OF TIME

Aside from Velcro, time is the most mysterious substance in the universe. You can't see it or touch it, yet a plumber can charge you upwards of seventy-five dollars per hour for it, *without necessarily fixing anything.*

Human beings first became aware of time during the era of the ancient Egyptians, who, while getting ready to build the Pyramids, invented the fundamental time unit, which is still in regular use today: the weekend. "We'll build those pyramids first thing after the weekend," the Egyptians were fond of saying, although of course when the weekend ended, they'd immediately start another one because it was the only unit they had. This was the Golden Age, and it was marked by the invention of beer.

The Golden Age ended tragically with the discovery of Wednesday, which led to the modern calendar featuring Friday, Tuesday, Pork Awareness Month, etc. This was followed by three major time advances:

- *Sometime*, which is a scientific unit of measurement meaning "in approximately 43 hillion jillion years," as in "Let's have lunch sometime!"
- *Daylight Savings Time*, which originated as a prank played by government employees who wanted to see if they could get an entire nation to change all its clocks twice a year without having the faintest idea why.
- *Military Time*, which is when you say things like "1400 hours." This is very useful for making brisk and efficient military statements, as in: "It took the squadron 1400 hours to deploy the \$4.2-million Mobile Laser-Enhanced Tactical Field Latrine, and it still flushes backward."

Today, more and more households are operating on Blink Time. This is when a power outage causes all the digital clocks in all of your appliances to blink "00:00," sometimes for months, because you can't figure out how to make them stop because the owner's manuals are totally unintelligible because all the actual instructions have been replaced by pages upon pages of lawyer-excreted statements beginning with the word WARNING. We've been on Blink Time in our household for as long as I can remember, and I've adjusted to it pretty well. I'm always looking at the microwave oven and saying, "Huh! It's 00:00 already! Time for a beer!" This is only one of the ways that I use time management to keep my life "on track," and you can, too, by following these:

PROVEN TIME-MANAGEMENT TECHNIQUES

When we talk about people who knew how to manage their time, the name that immediately springs to our lips, sometimes chipping our teeth, is Leonardo ("Leon the Vinci") da Vinci, a man who not only painted the famous *Mona Lisa,* but also, over the course of an incredibly prolific career, wrote Dante's *Inferno* and invented the Sony Walkman, not to mention accomplishing countless other accomplishments that would really amaze you if I had time to look them up.

How was Leonardo able to accomplish all this? His "secret" was actually the same basic, simple time-management technique that was also used by Alexander the Great, Benjamin Franklin, Thomas Jefferson, and many others who were famous for their productivity: *He never talked on the telephone.* "Tell them I'm in a meeting," he always used to say to his secretary (who, fortunately, spoke English). Because Leonardo knew that nothing on earth wastes time like a telephone.

This is a problem dating back to the very first telephone call, which, as you remember from elementary school, occurred when Alexander Graham Bell needed his assistant, Watson, so he invented the telephone and called him up. But what you *didn't* learn in school was that *Watson wasn't there.* He was out working on a case with Sherlock Holmes, so Bell had to invent the first telephone message slip and leave it on Watson's desk and sit around for hours, waiting for a return call, until finally he ducked out for a sandwich, which is of course when Watson called back, and they ended up leaving messages back and forth for weeks, and when they finally *did* get in touch with each other they felt obligated to exchange pleasantries, talk about sports, and tell jokes for fifteen minutes, during which they were repeatedly interrupted by loud, irritating clicks caused by Nazi scientists who at that time were perfecting the popular "call waiting" feature. By the time Bell and Watson finally got to the actual purpose of their conversation, neither one had the vaguest recollection of what it was.

That's what the telephone does: sucks the time right out of your life. You see these people driving around, talking on their car telephones, and you think, "Gosh, that must be *efficient*, having a car phone." What you don't realize is that some of these people have been stuck in those cars, glued to the damned phone, for *months,* surviving on drive-thru food and peeing in the ashtray. You want to go the *opposite* direction. You want to *dephone* your life to the maximum extent possible. The key is to remember this Efficiency Rule:

Never use the telephone to actually talk to people. Use it only to return their messages, comparable to the way a tennis player returns a serve.

"Here, take your damned message back," is the concept you are trying to convey. This is why it's very important that you call people back only when you're fairly sure they won't be there, such as lunchtime or Thanksgiving. Even then, you have to be alert in case you're dealing with a slippery customer who's actually *there:*

> YOU: Hello, I'm returning Mr. Leonard Prongmaker's call.
>
> PERSON ON THE OTHER END: This is Leonard Prong-maker.
>
> YOU: Okay, then, I'll try again another time. (Hang up briskly.)

You can also cut down drastically on incoming messages by unplugging your answering machine. (If you don't have one, you should buy one, *then* unplug it.)

Another excellent tip for saving time in the business environment is: never attend a meeting. Meetings are an addictive, highly self-indulgent activity that corporations and other large organizations habitually engage in only because they cannot actually masturbate. Nothing productive has ever happened in a meeting. If Noah had formed an Ark Construction Task Force, it would still be arguing over the ideal number of cubits. The federal government is basically one enormous, ongoing Meeting From Hell. Meetings are so inefficient that many major corporations are now staffing them entirely with temporary employees who are specially trained in what to do at meetings, namely not snore out loud. This frees the regular employees to get on with the vital work of attempting to return phone messages.

You can also save time by making your domestic routines more efficient. My son, for example, never turns off lights or closes the refrigerator door, thus saving several valuable nanoseconds per year. My wife and I avoid those long, time-consuming trips to the supermarket by buying our food in small quantities over the course of thirty to forty trips per week to convenience stores with names like the Way-Mor Expensive Food 'n' Microbe Mart. We even save time with our two dogs by frequently addressing them both by the same name ("NO!").

Using proven time-management techniques like these, I have transformed myself into a regular productivity machine, operating with the smooth precision of a fine Swiss watch that has been run over repeatedly by a coal train. The key to my efficiency is my daily schedule, a miracle of smart planning and split-second timing:

DAILY SCHEDULE

6:00 A.M.—Alarm goes off.
6:10, 6:20, 6:30, 6:40, 6:50 A.M.—Alarm goes off.
7:00 A.M.—Wake up and mentally review Plan of
    Action for accomplishing Today's Target Tasks.
7:10 A.M.—Alarm goes off.
7:11 A.M.—Open bedroom door and greet dogs.

(NOTE: I always allow at least ten minutes for this, because dogs have the same IQ as artichokes, and thus when they see me close the door at night—even though they've seen me do this approximately 1,300 times—they are certain they'll never see me again, and consequently they give me an insanely joyful welcome comparable to the one given to the Allied forces when they liberated Paris, the difference being that the Parisians were slightly less likely, in their enthusiasm, to pee on your feet.)

7:21 A.M.—Wake up child.

7:25 A.M.—Commence bathroom activities, including intense 12-minute inspection and tentative probing of impending nose zit.

7:45 A.M.—Wake up child.

7:48 A.M.—Prepare breakfast of modern, easy-to-prepare, nutrition-free food substances, such as Waffles In A Can.

7:50 A.M.—Wake up child.

8:00 A.M.—Read newspaper. Save time by skipping stories whose headlines contain any of the following words: NATO, ECONOMY, DOLLAR, MIDEAST, ENVIRONMENT, FEDERAL, OZONE, ASIA, PRESIDENT, CONGRESS, NUCLEAR, and CANCER. If running late, go directly to comics.

8:03 A.M.—Wake up child.

8:06 A.M.—Feed child quick breakfast consisting of cereal advertised on Saturday-morning television cartoon shows, such as Sug-a-Rama with Lumps o' Honey ("The Cereal That Makes Your Attention Span Even Shorter").

8:12 A.M.—Rush to car and drive child to school, learning en route that child's Science Fair project, which child has never mentioned, is due that morning.

8:23 A.M.—Arrive at school with completed Science Fair project, entitled "Objects Found in 1984 Jeep Ashtray."

8:25 A.M.—Drive to office, turning "dead time" in car to productive use by examining nose zit in rearview mirror and making helpful corrective gestures at other drivers.

9:07 A.M.—Arrive at office and immediately plunge into the hectic but invigorating task of getting coffee.

9:14 A.M.—Meet with co-workers to review issues left unresolved from previous day concerning pathetic state of Miami Dolphin defense.

9:37 A.M.—Coffee.

9:43 A.M.—Receive phone call from school official wondering how come child is not wearing shoes.

9:49 A.M.—Turn on word processor in preparation for day's highest-priority Target Task, writing humor column due several days earlier.

9:51 A.M.—Coffee.

10:20 A.M.—Stop in office of colleague for briefing concerning the story about the Polish airliner that crashed in a cemetery. (NOTE: They recovered 11,000 bodies.)

10:56 A.M.—Lunch.

11:27 A.M.—Back to work on humor column. Develop strong opening phrase: "One thing that has always struck me as very funny is . . ." Sink back in chair in exhaustion due to creative effort.

11:34 A.M.—Lunch.

12:22 P.M.—Review Polish airliner story with various colleagues.

1:34 P.M.—Revise opening phrase to read: "A very funny thing, and one that lends itself quite naturally to being the topic of a humor column, is . . ."

2:05 P.M.—Lunch.

2:42 P.M.—Come up with very strong new opening phrase: "If you're going to write a funny column, probably the easiest topic you could pick is . . ."

3:32 P.M.—Coffee.

3:51 P.M.—Nose zit update.

4:23 P.M.—Brief additional colleagues on Polish airliner matter.

4:47 P.M.—Lunch.

5:08 P.M.—Make final revisions to opening column phrase ("A humor-column topic so obvious that it practically writes itself is . . .").

5:27 P.M.—Explain to editor that only minor "fine-tuning" remains and column will definitely be finished by next day or following summer at latest.

6:39 P.M.—Arrive home to insanely joyful greeting from dogs, who, believing themselves abandoned forever, spent entire day throwing up in despair.

7:22 P.M.—Finish cleanup and commence quiet, intimate, romantic microwave pizza dinner with spouse.

7:23 P.M.—Receive phone call from school official with talent for sarcasm, inquiring about any possible plans in near future to pick up child.

7:52 P.M.—Return home with child to discover that dogs, grief-stricken over most recent departure, have managed to get pizza smears as high as seven feet up on living-room walls.

8:51 P.M.—Enjoy wholesome fast-food family dinner at Cholesterol Castle.

9:47 P.M.—Return home and enjoy emotional dog reunion resulting in several hairline fractures.

10:23 P.M.—Put child to bed and experience touching parental moment when, just as he is falling asleep, child remembers that on following day he is supposed to come to school in authentic costume of Yap islander.

10:32 P.M.—Nose zit update.

10:47 P.M.—Lunch.

11:00 P.M.—Turn on late news.

11:01 P.M.—Turn off late news when announcer uses word "nuclear."

11:02 P.M.—Sex life.

11:03 P.M.—Think about Target Tasks for tomorrow. Lots to do. Got column to write. Got developing nose zit. Got dogs to kill. Better set alarm for 6:00 A.M. sharp.

Of course, not every day goes as smoothly as this. Some days, despite my organizational efforts, unforeseen problems arise. Just today, for example, a couple of things came up at the last minute, and I never did get around to figuring out

NOTE: FIRST THING TOMORROW, THINK OF A CLEVER ENDING FOR THIS CHAPTER.

9

WISE FINANCIAL PLANNING FOR IRRESPONSIBLE SCUM SUCH AS YOURSELF

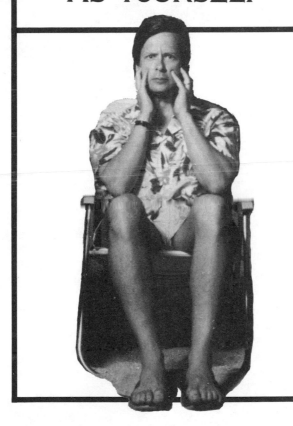

To understand the importance of financial planning for your retirement years, let's consider the famous true Aesop's fable about the grasshopper and the ant.

It seems that many years ago, there lived a lazy grasshopper and a hardworking ant. All summer long, while the ant was busily networking with other ants and gathering food, the grasshopper sat around drinking vodka gimlets and watching "General Hospital." When winter came, the grasshopper had nothing to eat, while the ant was snug and warm in his cozy little house filled with putrefying chunks of road-kill raccoon. Finally the grasshopper, starving, came to the ant's door and said, "Can I have some food?" And the ant said: "Well, I suppose GAACCKK," and they were both crushed by rocks dropped on them by Boy Scouts on a nature walk. This was a very poor financial decision, when you think how much money these boys could have gotten for a pair of talking insects.

As a person in your forties, you definitely want to avoid this kind of foolish financial decision, because the odds are that you'll be earning a paycheck for only about twenty more years, and even less if your employer realizes how often you use the Xerox machine for personal documents. This means that your future standard of living depends on the investments you make *today* (Wednesday). If you fail to plan ahead, you could well spend your retirement years eating dumpster food and living under a highway overpass. Whereas if you heed the advice outlined in this chapter, you'll be able to spend your "golden years" in a modern, state-of-the-art appliance carton. The choice is yours!

And let's not forget about financing your children's future educational needs. As you are no doubt aware, tuition costs have skyrocketed in recent years and are currently running as high as $15,000, sometimes even $20,000, per semester. And that's for nursery school. College is even worse. And yet, as a concerned parent, you want to make sure that your child does receive the benefits of a college education, to acquire the vital knowledge and skills that *you* acquired in college, such as how to take notes while sleeping, or drink bourbon through your nose. Yes, you want your child to have these advantages, but how can you afford it? Experts predict that by the year 2000 you'll have to pay $178 million just to put your child through a *bad* college, a college with a team nickname like "The Fighting Room Fresheners." Where are you going to get that kind of money? The only logical solution is to *rob college treasurers at gunpoint.*

No! Sorry! What I meant to say was that the only logical solution is to get yourself on a sensible investment program. Of course, I can't give you any specific investment advice without having detailed knowledge of your current financial situation. So let's start off by taking a close look at your investment portfolio. Let's see here . . . Hey! Wait a minute! *This* isn't an investment portfolio! This is your fifth-grade science project, entitled "How Worms Eat." Ha ha! Nice try, but you might as well admit it—you don't even *have* an investment portfolio. You've spent virtually all the money you've ever earned on basic necessities of life such as mortgages, car payments, pediatricians, plumbing, rental movies, take-out Chinese food, thousands of toys and accessories (sold separately), and untold millions of AA batteries (not included). You have nothing to show for all the money you've earned over the past twenty years except a heavily mortgaged house; a car that you owe twenty-seven more payments on, even though it's already showing symptoms of Fatal Transmission Disease; numerous malfunctioning appliances; huge mounds of books you never read, records you never listen to, clothes you never wear, and membership cards to health clubs you never go to; and—somewhere in the depths of your refrigerator—a year-old carton half-filled with a substance that may once have been mu-shu pork. Currently your major tangible financial asset is a coffee can containing seventeen pounds of loose change, much of it Canadian.

So your financial situation is a mess. Okay, fine. The important thing is—*don't be discouraged.* There's no reason to get down on yourself, just because you've been an unbelievable jerk. The important thing is to get yourself straightened out *now*, with Step One being to track your "cash flow" to determine where your money comes from, where it goes, whether it's having an affair, etc. Odds are you'll find out that you have what economists call:

THE NORMAL HUMAN CASH FLOW
(With Key Terms in Boldface)

Money comes from the **bank,** *which puts it in the* **automatic** *teller, from which it flows into your* **wallet,** *at which point* **UFO Rays from Space** *cause all the money to* **disappear** *so* **mysteriously** *that you often remark upon it to your* **spouse,** *as in: "I don't understand it! I had forty-seven dollars in my wallet this morning and all I bought was* **gas** *and some* **guacamole dip** *and now it [meaning the money] [also the guacamole dip] is all* **gone!"** *So you go back to the* **automatic bank teller** *to see if there's any* **more money,** *which there probably is* **not** *because your last* **credit-card statement** *showed that you had gone way over your* **credit limit** *due to* **several dozen ludicrously unnecessary purchases** *that you apparently made while under the influence of* **powerful narcotics,** *such as the purchase totaling* **$168.92** *from a place called* **Spatula World,** *the result being that you had to write a* **fairly massive check** *to the* **Visa Corporation,** *which is hooked up somehow with the* **bank,** *and which you hope will get your money and put some of it back in the* **automatic teller** *soon so you can get it back* **out** *again because you already need more* **gas.**

Of course, your individual mileage may vary. But we can see from this analysis that the only way you'll be able to save for your retirement years will be if you put yourself on a regular savings plan wherein the first thing you do whenever you get some money is to take a certain amount away from yourself, by force if necessary, and put it to work for you by means of a simple investment strategy. The simplest strategy I know of is the one we use in our household, which we call:

THE WEALTH-THROUGH-SICKNESS INVESTMENT PROGRAM

Here's how it works:

1. Every week, rain or shine, one or more of us gets sick and we go to the doctor's office and pay varying amounts of money in exchange for finding out that we are sick.
2. Every six or eight months, whichever comes later, I sit down at the kitchen table with huge piles of medical receipts and attempt to fill out my medical insurance claim forms, which, in the honored tradition of forms, have apparently been designed by people with severe disorders of the attention span. The questions go like this:
   1. What is your name?
   2. What is the patient's name?
   3. Are you the same as the patient? (If "no," then who is?)
   4. What was your name again?
3. Several weeks later, the insurance company mails us a check and an explanation written in extremely

clear language, although unfortunately not English ("This amount reflects your total coverage exposure MINUS your accrued deductible TIMES your applicable exemptions PLUS your windfall profits tax DIVIDED BY the cosine of your . . ." etc.). Sometimes we get back as much as 70 percent of our money (called the "rate of return," or "Fanny Mae"), which we then wisely reinvest in doctors' fees, unless we're running low on beer.

The advantage of the Wealth-Through-Sickness Investment Program is that it's virtually automatic. The disadvantage is that the only person who becomes wealthy is the doctor. You, on the other hand, gradually become poorer, and probably also fatter, depending on your beer consumption. So if you're looking to actually *increase* the amount of money you have, my advice would be to get yourself into a sound, stable, diversified, long-term investment program of betting on dog races. Unless, of course, you're more of a risk-taker, in which case you could put your money into a savings-and-loan institution, which is kind of like a bank except it has boards on the windows. Or, if you're a *real* gambler, you might want to consider investing in:

THE STOCK MARKET

The way this works is, you find yourself a reputable stockbroker (defined as "a stockbroker who has not been indicted yet"), and you give him some money. He keeps some for himself and uses the rest to buy you a stock that he got a Hot Tip on and Recommends Highly, although of course he keeps his own personal money in a mayonnaise jar. Next you spend a lot of time trying to keep track of your stock by frowning at the newspaper financial listings, which look like this:

	UP	ODDS	RBI	VCR	LOW TIDE	EAST
Gmrh	34	4–3	23	$349	3:43	One Spade
Sodm	12	8–1	8(e)	45% off	IRT #2	No Trumps

You also spend a lot of time listening to radio and TV "financial analysts" who clearly have no idea what the stock market is going to do next, but are absolutely brilliant at coming up with creative explanations as to why it did whatever it just did. ("Stocks were off sharply today in response to rumors that the July unemployment figures have been eaten by goats.") Eventually you start to notice that your "can't-miss" stock is not performing up to expectations, as evidenced by the fact that the newspaper is now listing it on the comics page. Finally you tell your broker to sell it, which he does, taking another chunk of the proceeds for himself and paying the balance to you out of one of those bus-driver-style change dispensers. Then he's off to the golf course, to pick up some more Hot Tips for you.

Aside from providing your stockbroker with a steady income, another important objective of your long-term investment strategy is to feel a constant nagging guilt about:

LIFE INSURANCE

How do you know whether you have enough life insurance? How can you be sure that if, God forbid, something terrible were to happen to you, your loved ones would be able to continue squandering money in the manner to which they have become accustomed? I put this question to the Life Insurance Institute, which provided this:

HELPFUL SELF-TEST QUESTIONNAIRE TO SEE IF YOU HAVE ENOUGH LIFE INSURANCE
(Sponsored by the Life Insurance Institute)

1. How much insurance do you have?_____
2. You need more.
3. We'll send somebody over right now.

Of course, no discussion of your financial future would be complete without some mention of the terrific retirement program dreamed up by the federal government, which is the same shrewd financially savvy outfit that gave us the $600 military toilet seat. I refer, of course, to:

SOCIAL SECURITY

The way this works is: the government takes an ever-larger chunk of money out of your paycheck and gives it to retired people, even the ones who already have a whole lot more money than you do and use their social security checks exclusively to purchase sun hats for their racehorses. But you continue to pay, because you're a generous, caring person who does not wish to be thrown into jail. Also you figure that someday *you'll* retire, and you'll get back all the money you paid in. The flaw in this reasoning is that when our whole humongously over-sized generation retires, there's going to be virtually no work force left to support us. The government will be trying to suck billions of dollars every week out of an estimated fifty-three teenage Burger King employees. It's not going to work. The whole social security system is going to come crashing down, and you're not going to get a nickel, which is okay because there won't be anything to buy anyway, once the Greenhouse Effect causes the polar ice caps to melt to the point where the shopping malls are patronized mainly by jellyfish, assuming that all life on the planet hasn't already been wiped out by toxic waste or nuclear war, which could of course break out at any moment, which is why I can't stress enough the importance of getting started *today* on your long-term financial planning. Me, I'm going to order some Chinese food.

10

POLITICS AFTER 40: YOU DON'T NEED A WEATHERMAN TO KNOW THAT HARSH SUNLIGHT CAN HARM YOUR BMW'S FINISH

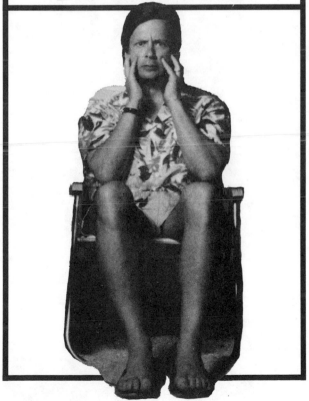

ou hardly ever see radical activists anymore. The last time I saw any up close was at the 1988 Democratic convention in Atlanta, the one where the Democrats nominated Michael "The Human Quaalude" Dukakis. The Democrats had thoughtfully set up a Designated Protest Area right next to the convention hall. (This was in stark contrast to the Republicans, who held *their* convention right next to—this is true—a shopping center.)

The Democrats' Designated Protest Area featured a powerful public-address system and a stage where, according to the official protest schedule, various groups or individuals would get up and make long, impassioned speeches for or against endangered crustaceans or transvestite canoeists' rights or whatever, their voices booming out from the huge speakers and thundering across a listening throng averaging maybe nine people, seven of whom were waiting for their turn to protest.

The protesters who showed up most often, sometimes interrupting other people's protests, were a group of left-wing radical activists. They were mostly kids in their teens or early twenties. Fashion-wise, they favored a sportswear look that I would call "Pretend Guerrilla," sometimes including bandannas pulled up over their faces, thus enabling them to blend into the downtown Atlanta environment as unobtrusively as water buffalo at a formal wedding. They communicated almost exclusively by shouting slogans, and their philosophy boiled down to two basic points:

1. They represented The People.
2. They hated people.

At least that's the way it seemed, because they were always in a spittle-emitting rage, loudly accusing everybody they encountered—police, other protesters, media people, spectators, trash cans, squirrels—of being mother-f-wording CIA fascists. They used this expression reflexively, the way supermarket cashiers use "Have a nice day."

Needless to say, the radicals were very persuasive. After a few minutes of listening to them shout in your face, you were ready to march down to the CIA Recruitment Center and sign up. At least I was, and this bothered me somewhat. Because, like almost everybody in my generation except Julie Nixon and David Eisenhower, I used to be a left-wing, antiestablishment, protest-oriented, march-on-Washington type of individual. Once, back in college, I even participated in a hunger strike to end the Vietnam War. By not eating, I was supposedly enabling myself to focus my consciousness on peace. What actually happened was that I became absolutely obsessed with cheeseburgers, although if I really, really forced myself to concentrate on the tragedy in Southeast Asia, I could also visualize french fries. I kept this up for several days, but failed to have much of an impact on Washington. At no point, as far as I know, did a White House aide burst into the Oval Office and shout with alarm, "Some students at Haverford College have been refusing to eat for several days!" followed by Lyndon Johnson saying, "Mah God! Ah got to change mah foreign policy!"

But the point is, at least I was *trying,* in my own naïve and painfully earnest way, to do what I thought was the right thing. Whereas these days I never seem to get involved in causes. The last time I remember protesting anything with any real passion was when I was at a professional basketball game and the arena management decided to stop selling beer in the fourth quarter.

Of course, some would argue that, hey, the war is over, so there aren't any causes to get involved in anymore. Which is of course ridiculous. There are all *kinds* of causes to be alarmed about. For example, there's the Greenhouse Effect, which is one of the more recent in a series of alarming worldwide homicidal trends to be discovered by those busy beavers, the scientists. They've found that the Earth is slowly being turned into a vast greenhouse, so that by the year 2010—unless something is done—the entire human race will be crushed beneath a humongous tomato.

Or something along those lines. I confess that I haven't been following the Greenhouse Effect all that closely. Whenever I'm reading the newspaper and I come to the words "Greenhouse Effect," I continue reading, but I squinch my eyes up real tight so that the words become a meaningless blur. I originally developed this technique for watching suspense movies, in which the characters wander around inside a house with menacing background music and nothing happens and nothing happens and nothing happens and nothing happens and *my God it plucked her eyeballs out like a pair of grapes.*

I'm not saying that the Greenhouse Effect is not extremely important. Hey, I live in Miami, and if the polar ice caps start melting, I stand a good chance of waking up one morning and finding myself festooned with kelp. It's just that, what with working and paying bills and transporting my son to and from the pediatrician and trying to teach the dog not to throw up on the only nice rug in the entire house, I just don't seem to have enough room in my brain for the Greenhouse Effect and all the other problems I know I should be concerned about, such as drugs and AIDS and Lebanon and pollution and cholesterol and caffeine and cancer and Japanese investors buying the Lincoln Memorial and nuclear war and dirty rock lyrics and this new barbecue grill we got. Our old grill rusted out. It was your basic model, the kind where you put your charcoal in, you lit it, you noticed about an hour later that the charcoal had gone out, and you ordered a pizza. It gave us many years of good service.

Our new grill was purchased by my wife, Beth, who would be a natural in the field of military procurement because whatever she's buying, she always gets the most fangled one they sell. She came home with a grill approx-

imately the size of a nuclear submarine but more compli-
cated, featuring knobs, valves, switches, auto-ignite, a
fold-down side table, "flavor bars," a side burner, an
electric rotisserie, and much more. This grill squats out
on the patio, the lord of all it surveys. For weeks I was
afraid to go near it. Finally I decided, hey, it's just a grill,
so I got out the owner's manual, which is twenty-eight
pages long. Here's what it says:

CAUTION! (five times)
DANGER! (six times)
WARNING! (thirty-eight times)

These are true statistics. So we are talking about a total
of forty-nine scary things to remember just about a barbecue grill, and, frankly, I do not feel up to it. The only
warning I even started to read was on page 3, which
begins, I swear, with the words:

WARNING!!!!!
SPIDER AND INSECT ALERT

This is followed by the statement: "Your Genesis Gas
Barbecue as well as any outdoor gas appliance is a target
for spiders and insects." Needless to say, I stopped reading right there, because the very thought of insects tar-
geting my grill (For what? Theft?) makes me want to get
into the fetal position.

My point is that whereas I once felt totally confident
of my ability to shape the destiny of the nation and, yes,
the world, I now have grave doubts about my ability to

cope with a patio appliance. Aside from giving my Fair Share to the United Fund, I have pretty much withdrawn from causes, and so, apparently, have many other members of my generation, except perhaps for David and Julie Nixon Eisenhower, who, being 180 degrees out of sync, are probably living in a geodesic dome somewhere, smoking hashish by the kilogram and making plans to blow up the Pentagon.

Sometimes I think I'd like to get more involved politically, but I get depressed when I look at the two major name-brand political parties. Both of them seem to be dominated by the kind of aggressively annoying individuals who always came in third for sophomore class president. Which is not to say that there are no differences between the parties. The Democrats seem to be basically nicer people, but they have demonstrated time and again that they have the management skills of celery. They're the kind of people who'd stop to help you change a flat, but would somehow manage to set your car on fire. I would be reluctant to entrust them with a Cuisinart, let alone the economy. The Republicans, on the other hand, would know how to fix your tire, but they wouldn't bother to stop because they'd want to be on time for Ugly Pants Night at the country club. Also, the Republicans have a high Beady-Eyed Self-Righteous Scary Borderline Loon Quotient, as evidenced by Phyllis Schlafly, Pat Robertson, the entire state of Utah, etc.

But the biggest problem I have with both major political parties is that they seem to be competing in some kind of giant national scavenger hunt every four years to see who can find the biggest goober to run for President.

I was hoping that things would improve when my generation took over—when somebody my age, representing the best that my generation had to offer, morally and intellectually, got nominated to a national ticket. When this finally happened, of course, the nod went to "Dan" Quayle, a man whose concept of visionary leadership is steering his own golf cart, a man who—and I mean no disrespect when I say this—would not stand out, intellectually, in a vat of plankton.

I can hear you saying: "Oh yeah, Mr. Smartass? Well, what kind of leader would *you* be?" The answer is, I'd be a terrible leader. I'd be such an inadequate leader that within a matter of days the United States would rank significantly below Belize as a world power. But at least I'd try to be an *interesting* leader. I wouldn't be one more pseudo-somber, blue-suited, red-tied, wingtip-shoed weenie, frowning at the issues with sincerely feigned concern. I'd try to truly represent my generation, the rock-'n'-roll generation that had the idealism and courage to defy the Establishment, stand up for what it believed in, march in the streets and go to Woodstock and sleep in the rain and become infested with body lice. If I were the President, I'd bring some *life* to the White House. The theme of my administration would be summarized by the catchy and inspirational phrase: "Hey, The Government Is Beyond Human Control, So Let's at Least Have Some Fun with It." Here are some of the specific programs I would implement:

- I would invite George Thorogood and the Delaware Destroyers to perform at the White House. Not just once. *Every night.* They would *live* there. Congress would constantly be passing Joint Resolutions urging the Executive Branch to keep the volume down.

- Whenever I entered the room for a formal dinner, the band would play the 1963 Angels' hit, "My Boyfriend's Back."
- I would propose that the government launch a $17-billion War on Light Beer.
- I would have a Labrador retriever, wearing a small earphone, sit in on all Cabinet meetings.
- I would request a summit meeting with the Soviet Premier, at which I would make a dramatic three-hour presentation, using flip-charts, of the benefits of becoming an Amway distributor.
- One of my highest priorities would be to have helium declared the National Element.
- I would awaken key congressional leaders at 2:30 one morning and summon them to the White House Situation Room for an urgent meeting, at which, after swearing them to secrecy, I would show them a top-secret spy-satellite photograph revealing that China is shaped vaguely like an eggplant.
- The cornerstone of my foreign policy would be playing pranks on France.
- Wherever I went, there would be a burly Secret Service man just a few feet away, and on his wrist would be a handcuff, which would be attached to a steel chain, which would be attached to a locked steel carrying case, and inside that case would be: an Etch-a-Sketch.

HOW TO TELL IF YOU'RE TURNING INTO A REPUBLICAN

It's very common for people reaching middle age to turn into Republicans. It can happen overnight. You go to bed as your regular old T-shirt-wearing self, and you wake up the next morning with Ralph Lauren clothing and friends named Muffy. Here are some other signs to watch for:

- You find yourself judging political candidates solely on the basis of whether or not they'd raise your taxes. "Well," you say, "he *was* convicted in those machete slayings, but at least he won't raise my taxes."
- You assign a lower priority to ending world hunger than to finding a cleaning lady.
- You start clapping wrong to music.

The last item above is something I've noticed about Republicans at their conventions. The band will start playing something vaguely upbeat—a real GOP rocker such as "Bad, Bad LeRoy Brown"—and the delegates will decide to get funky and clap along, and it immediately becomes clear that they all suffer from a tragic Rhythm Deficiency, possibly caused by years of dancing the bunny hop to bands with names like "Leon Wudge and His Sounds of Clinical Depression." To determine whether Republican Rhythm Impairment Syndrome is afflicting you, you should take the Ray Charles Clapping Test. All you do is hum the song "Hit the Road, Jack" and clap along. A rhythmically normal person will clap as follows:

"Hit the road, (CLAP) Jack (CLAP)."

Whereas a Republican will clap this way:

"Hit the (CLAP), (CLAP)."

(By the way, if you don't even *know* the song "Hit the Road, Jack," then not only are you a Republican, but you might even be Cabinet material.)

I'll tell you what's weird. Not only is our generation turning into Republicans, but we also have a whole generation coming after us who are *starting out* as Republicans. With the exception of the few dozen spittle-emitting radicals I saw in Atlanta, the younger generations today are already so conservative they make William F. Buckley, Jr., look like Ho Chi Minh. What I'm wondering is, what will they be like when they're our age? Will they, too, change their political philosophy? Will millions of young urban professionals turn 40 and all of a sudden start turning into left-wing, antiestablishment hippies, smoking pot on the racquetball court, putting Che Guevera posters up in the conference room, and pasting flower decals all over their cellular telephones? It is an exciting time to look forward to. I plan to be dead.

11

SPORTS FOR THE OVER-40 PERSON (OR, GOD HAD A *REASON* FOR CREATING THE BARCALOUNGER)

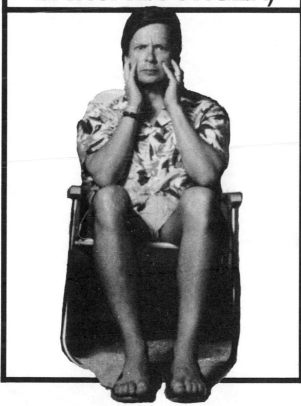

In the Pantheon of Sports Heroes (which is located next to the Skeet-Shooting Hall of Fame), you'll find the names of many legendary athletes who remained active in sports well after they turned 40—Babe Ruth, Jack Dempsey, Picasso, Secretariat—the list goes on and on.

What do these great competitors have in common? Right. They're all dead. So you see how important it is for you to slow down as you get older, to abandon the active sports you enjoyed so much in your youth—basketball, tennis, racquetball, drinking a quart of Jim Beam and leaping naked into the motel pool from the eighth-floor balcony, etc. It's time for you to start "acting your age" by getting involved in the kinds of sports activities that are more appropriate for mature, responsible adults, such as:

SHRIEKING AT LITTLE LEAGUERS

To participate in this highly popular sport, all you need to do is get a small child who would be infinitely happier just staying home and playing in the dirt, and put a uniform on this child and make him stand for hours out on a field with other reluctant children who are no more capable of hitting or catching or accurately throwing a baseball than they are of performing neurosurgery. Then you and the other grownups stand around the perimeter and leap up and down and shriek at these children as though the fate of the human race depended on their actions.

The object of the game is to activate your child if the ball goes near him, similar to the way you use levers to activate the little men in table-hockey games. Your child will be standing out in right field, picking his nose, staring into space, totally oblivious to the game, and the ball will come rolling his way, and your job is to leap violently up and down and shriek, "GET THE BALL! GET THE BALL!!" repeatedly for several minutes until your child finally is aroused from his reverie long enough to glance down and discover, to his amazement, the ball. The ball! Of all things! Right here in the middle of a Little League game! While your child is staring at the ball curiously, as if examining a large and unusual tropical insect, you switch to yelling: "THROW THE BALL! THROW THE BALL! THROWTHEBALL THROWTHEBALL THROWTHEBALL THROWTHEBALL THROWTHE BALL THROWTHEBALL! *THROW* THE BALL, DAMMIT!!" After several minutes of this an idea will start to form somewhere deep inside your child's brain: *Perhaps I should throw the ball.* Yes! It's crazy, but it just might work!

And so, seconds before you go into cardiac arrest on

the sidelines, your child will pick up the ball and hurl it, Little League–style, in a totally random direction, then resume picking his nose and staring off into space. As you collapse, exhausted, the ball will roll in the general direction of some *other* child, whose poor unfortunate parent must then try to activate *him*. Meanwhile, the *other* team's parents will be shrieking at *their* children to run around the bases in the correct direction. It is not uncommon for 150 runs to score on one Little League play. A single game can go on for weeks.

I get to engage in a lot of sideline-shrieking, because tragically we have very nice weather down here in South Florida, which means that while most of the nation enjoys the luxury of being paralyzed by slush, we subtropical parents are trapped in Year-Round Youth Sports Hell. The reason we have a high crime rate is that many parents are so busy providing transportation that they have to quit their jobs and support their families by robbing convenience stores on their way to practices, games, lessons, etc.

But at least our children are becoming well rounded. That's what I tell myself while I shriek at my son, who is out there in left field, watching commercial aircraft fly overhead while the ball rolls cheerfully past him and seven runners score. I tell myself that if my son were not out there participating in sports, he would not be learning one of life's most important lessons, namely: "It doesn't matter whether you win or lose, because you are definitely going to lose."

My son's teams lose a lot. This is because he is a Barry. We Barrys have a tradition of terrible sports luck dating back to my father, whose entire high-school football career—this is true—consisted of a single play, which was blocking a punt with his nose. As a child, I played on an unbroken succession of losing baseball teams, although "played" is probably too strong a term. My primary role was to sit on the bench, emitting invisible but potent Loser Rays and joining with the other zero-motor-control bench-sitters in thinking up hilarious and highly creative insults to hurl at members of the other team. Let's say the opposing batter was named Frank. We'd yell: "Hey, FRANK! What's your last name? *FURTER?*" Then we'd laugh so hard that we'd fall backward off the bench while Frank hit a triple, scoring twelve runs.

My son is a much better player than I was, but he's still a Barry, and consequently his teams generally lose. He was on one Little League team, the Red Sox, that lost at least 45,000 games in a span of maybe four months. Teams were coming from as far away as Guam to play the Red Sox. All of these teams complied with the First Law of Little League Physics, which states: "The other team always has much larger kids." You parents may have noticed that your child's team always consists of normal-sized, even puny, children, while the other team is always sponsored by Earl's House of Steroids.

So the Red Sox were constantly playing against huge, mutant 9-year-olds who had more bodily hair than I do and drove themselves to the game, and we were getting creamed. I served as a part-time first-base coach, and I spent a lot of time analyzing our technique, trying to pinpoint exactly what it was that we were doing wrong, and as best as I could figure it, our problem was that—

follow me closely here—*we never scored any runs.* Ever.

There was a good reason for this: The boys were not idiots. They did not wish to be struck by the ball. When they were batting, they looked perfect—good stance, fierce glare at the pitcher, professional-style batting glove, etc.—until the pitcher would actually pitch, at which point, no matter where the ball was going, the Red Sox batters would twitch their bodies violently backward like startled squids, the difference being that a squid would have a better chance of hitting the baseball because it keeps its eyes open.

Frankly, I didn't blame the boys. This was exactly the hitting technique that I used in Little League on those rare occasions when I got to play. But as a first-base coach I had a whole new perspective on the game, namely the perspective of a person who never had to get up to bat. So my job was to yell foolish advice to the batters. "Don't back up!" I'd yell. "He's not gonna hit you!" Every now and then a Red Sock, ignoring his common sense, would take me seriously and fail to leap backward, and of course when this happened the hormonally unbalanced, 275-pound pitcher always fired the ball directly into the batter's body. Then my job was to rush up and console the batter by telling him, "Legally, you cannot be forced to play organized baseball."

I'm just kidding, of course. Far be it from me to bring down the republic. What I'd say was, "Rub it off! Attaboy! Okay!" And the boy, having learned the important life lesson that adults frequently spout gibberish, would sniffle his way down to first base, while our next batter was silently resolving to be in a different area code by the time the ball reached home plate.

Speaking of coaching, this is an excellent way for the sports-oriented person to avoid the physical risks of actually participating physically in the sport, and yet still have the opportunity to experience the emotion and excitement of sudden heart failure. I coached my son's soccer team, the Phantoms, for one game. This was pretty ridiculous, because the only soccer rules I remembered, from junior high school, were:

1. You're allowed to hit the ball with your head.
2. But it hurts.

The way I was selected as coach was that the regular coach, Rick, was on vacation for two weeks, and the other parents decided that I was best qualified to be the substitute coach on account of I wasn't there when they decided this.

The Phantoms, needless to say, were a struggling team. In addition to being cursed by the Barry luck, they had been decimated by birthday parties, and they were not having a banner year in the sense of winning games or even necessarily getting the ball down the field far enough so the opposing goalkeeper had to stop picking his ear.

So I was concerned about being the coach. I had, of course, attended many soccer games over the years, but all I ever did was stand around with the other parents, randomly yelling, "KICK IT!" After I was elected substitute coach, I did attend a team practice in hopes of learning some strategy, but unfortunately this was the practice at which the Official Team Photograph was taken, which was very time-consuming because every time the photographer got the team posed, several players would be attacked by ants. Down here in South Florida we have highly aggressive ants, ants that draw no distinction between a cashew nut and a human being. You turn your back on them, and next thing you know, you hear this rhythmic ant work chant and your child is being dragged underground.

So the Phantoms spent most of the practice swatting at their legs and moving, gypsy-like, around the field, looking for an ant-free location, and the only thing they really practiced was getting into team-photograph formation. I did speak briefly with Rick, who gave me the following coaching pointers:

1. The game starts at 1:30.

He also gave me a coach-style clipboard and some official league literature on Soccer Theory, which I attempted to read about an hour before game time. Unfortunately, it was not designed to be read by desperate, unprepared fathers. It was designed to be read by unusually smart nuclear physicists. It starts out with these handy definitions:

a. Principles of Play: the rules of action (guidelines) that support the basic objectives of soccer.
b. Tactics: the means by which the principles or rules are executed.

c. Strategy: which tactics are to be used, the
arrangement of . . .

And so on. I read these words several times, gradually
becoming convinced that they'd make equal sense to me
in any order. They could say: "Strategy: the tactics by
which the rules (principles) support the execution." Or,
"Principles: the strategic (tactical) arrangement of exec-
utives wearing supporters."

So you can imagine how well prepared I felt when I
arrived at the soccer field. The Phantoms gathered
around me, awaiting leadership. Nearby, our opponents,
looking like the Brazilian national team, only larger,
were running through some snappy pre-game drills. The
Phantoms looked at them, then looked at me expec-
tantly. My brain, working feverishly under pressure,
began to form a shrewd coaching concept, a tactic by
which we might be able to execute the guidelines of our
strategy.

"Okay!" I announced. "Let's run some pre-game
drills!"

The Phantoms, showing rare unity of purpose, re-
sponded immediately. "We don't have a ball," they
pointed out. There was nothing about this in the coaching materials.

Next it was time for the Pre-game Talk. "Okay, Phantoms!" I shouted. "Gather 'round! Listen up!"

The Phantoms gathered 'round. They listened up.
Suddenly it occurred to me that I had nothing whatsoever to tell them.

"Okay!" I said. "Let's go!"

The game itself is a blur in my memory. My strategy—yelling "KICK IT!"—did not seem to be effective. The other team, which at times appeared to be playing with as many as four balls, was scoring on us regularly. We were not scoring at all. We were having trouble just executing the play where you run without falling down. As the situation deteriorated, I approached some of the other fathers on the sidelines. "What do you think we should do?" I asked. They did not hesitate.

"We should go to a bar," they said.

In the third quarter I changed my strategy from yelling "KICK IT!" to yelling "WAY TO GO!" This had no effect on anything, but I felt better. Finally the game ended, and I attempted to console the Phantoms over their heartbreaking loss. But they were beyond consolation. They were already into racing around, pouring Gatorade on each other. I'm sure they'll eventually overcome the trauma of this loss. Whereas I will probably never again be able to look at a clipboard without whimpering.

Probably the fastest-growing sport for the over-40 person is one that combines the advantages of a good cardiovascular workout with the advantages of looking like you have a bizarre disorder of the central nervous system. I refer to:

WALKING LIKE A DORK

Walking like a dork has become very popular among older people who used to jog for their health but could no longer afford the orthopedic surgery. The object of dork-walking is to make a simple, everyday act performed by millions of people every day, namely walking, look as complex and strenuous as Olympic pole-vaulting. To do this, you need to wear a special outfit, including high-tech, color-coordinated shorts and sweat-clothes and headbands and wristbands and a visor and a Sony Walkperson tape player and little useless weights for your hands and special dork-walking shoes that cost as much per pair as round-trip airfare to London.

But the most important thing is your walking technique. You have to make your arms and legs as stiff as possible and swing them violently forward and back in an awkward, vaguely Richard Nixon–like manner. It helps a lot to have an enormous butt, waving around back there like the Fiji blimp in a tornado. You'll know you're doing it right when passing motorists laugh so hard that they drive into trees.

But as you age, you may find that even dork-walking is too strenuous for you. In this case, you'll want to look into the ultimate aging-person activity, a "sport" that requires so little physical activity that major tournaments are routinely won by coma victims. I refer, of course, to:

GOLF

Nobody knows exactly how golf got started. Probably what happened was, thousands of years ago, a couple of primitive guys were standing around, holding some odd-shaped sticks, and they noticed a golf ball lying on the grass, and they said, "Hey! Let's see if we can hit this into a hole!" And then they said, "Nah, let's just tell long, boring anecdotes about it instead."

Which is basically the object, in golf. You put on the most unattractive pants that money can buy, pants so ugly that they have to be manufactured by blind people in dark rooms, and you get together in the clubhouse with other golfers and drone away for hours about how you "bogeyed" your three-iron on the par six, or your six-iron on the par three, or whatever. Also you watch endless televised professional golf tournaments with names like the Buick Merrill Lynch Manufacturers Hanover Frito-Lay Ti-D-Bol Preparation H Classic, which consist entirely of moderately overweight men holding clubs and frowning into the distance while, in the background, two announcers hold interminable whispered conversations like this:

FIRST ANNOUNCER: Bob, he's lying about eighteen yards from the green with a fourteen-mile-per-hour wind out of the northeast, a relative humidity of seventy-two percent, and a chance of afternoon or evening thundershowers. He might use a nine-iron here.

SECOND ANNOUNCER: Or possibly an eight, Bill. Or even—this makes me so excited that I almost want to speak in a normal tone of voice—a seven.

FIRST ANNOUNCER: Or he could just keep on frowning into space. Remember that one time we had a professional golfer frown for five solid hours, never once hitting a ball, us whispering the whole time in between Buick commercials, and it turned out he'd had some kind of seizure and died, standing up, gripping his sand wedge?

SECOND ANNOUNCER: In that situation, Bill, I'd have used a putter.

If you *really* get into golf, you can actually try to play it some time, although this is not a requirement. I did it once, with a friend of mine named Paul, who is an avid golfer in the sense that if he had to choose between playing golf and ensuring permanent world peace, he'd want to know how many holes.

So we got out on the golf course in one of those little electric carts that golfers ride around in to avoid the danger that they might actually have to contract some muscle tissue. Also, we had an enormous collection of random clubs and at least 3,000 balls, which turned out to be not nearly enough.

The way we played was, first Paul would hit his ball directly toward the hole. This is basic golfing strategy: You want to hit the ball the least possible number of times so you can get back to the clubhouse to tell boring anecdotes and drink. When it was my turn, we'd drive the cart to wherever my ball was, which sometimes meant taking the interstate highway. When we finally arrived at our destination, Paul would examine the situation and suggest a club.

"Try a five-iron here," he'd say, as if he honestly believed it would make a difference.

Then, with a straight face, he'd give me very specific directions as to where I should hit the ball. "You want to aim it about two and a half yards to the right of that fourth palm tree," he'd say, pointing at a palm tree that I could not hit with a Strategic Defense Initiative laser. I'd frown, pro-golfer-style, at this tree, then I'd haul off and take a violent swing at the ball, taking care to keep my head down, which is an important part of your golf stroke because it gives you a legal excuse if the ball winds up lodged in somebody's brain.

Sometimes, after my swing, the ball would still be there, surrounded by a miniature scene of devastation, similar to the view that airborne politicians have of federal disaster areas. Sometimes the ball would be gone, which was the signal to look up and see how hard Paul was trying not to laugh. Usually he was trying very hard, which meant the ball had gone about as far as you would hide an Easter egg from a small child with impaired vision. But sometimes the ball had completely disappeared, and we'd look for it, but we'd never see it again. I think it went into another dimension, a parallel universe where people are still talking about the strange day when these golf balls started materializing out of thin air, right in the middle of dinner parties, concerts, etc.

So anyway, by following this golfing procedure, Paul and I were able to complete nine entire holes in less time than it would have taken us to memorize *Moby Dick* in Korean. We agreed that nine holes was plenty for a person with my particular level of liability insurance, so we headed back to the clubhouse for a beer, which, despite being a novice at golf, I was able to swallow with absolutely no trouble. The trick is to keep your head up.

Speaking of drinking beer, another sport that you'll want to get into as you get older is:

FISHING

Fishing is very similar to golf because in both sports you hold a long skinny thing in your hand while nothing happens for days at a time. The major advantage of fishing is that you are somewhat less likely to be killed by a golf ball; the disadvantage is that you have to become involved with bait, which consists of disgusting little creatures with a substance known to biologists as "bait glop" constantly oozing out of various orifices. The function of the bait is to be repulsive and thereby reduce the chances that a fish will bite it and wind up in your boat thrashing and gasping piteously and occasionally whispering, in a quiet but clear voice, "Please help me!" If you were to put a nice roast-beef sandwich on your hook, or an egg roll, you'd have fish coming from entirely different time zones to get caught. But not so with bait. "He's so dumb, he'd eat bait," is a common fish expression, which means that the only fish you're in any danger of catching are the total morons of the marine community, which is why, when you see them mounted on people's walls, they always have a vaguely vice-presidential expression. Not that I am naming names.

SKIING

If you're bored by slower activities such as fishing and golf, and you're looking for the kind of youth-recapturing, action-packed sport that offers you the opportunity to potentially knock down a tree with your face, you can't do better than skiing.

The key to a successful ski trip, of course, is planning, by which I mean *money*. For openers, you have to buy a special outfit that meets the strict requirements of the Ski Fashion Institute, namely:

1. It must cost as much as a medium wedding reception.
2. It must make you look like the Giant Radioactive Easter Bunny From Space.
3. It must be made of a mutant fiber with a name that sounds like the villain on a Saturday-morning cartoon show, such as "Gore-Tex," so as to provide the necessary resistance to moisture—which, trust me, will be gushing violently from all of your major armpits once you start lunging down the mountain.

You also have to buy ski goggles costing upwards of fifty dollars per eyeball that are specially designed not to not fog up under any circumstances except when you put them on, at which time they become approximately as transparent as the Los Angeles telephone directory, which is why veteran skiers recommend that you do not pull them down over your eyes until just before you make contact with the tree. And you'll need ski boots, which are made from melted bowling balls and which protect your feet by preventing your blood, which could contain dangerous germs, from traveling below your shins.

As for the actual skis, you should rent them, because of the feeling of confidence you get from reading the fine print on the lengthy legal document that the rental personnel make you sign, which is worded as follows: "The undersigned agrees that skiing is an INSANELY DANGEROUS ACTIVITY, and that the rental personnel were just sitting around minding their OWN BUSINESS when the undersigned, who agrees that he or she is a RAVING LOON, came BARGING IN UNINVITED, waving a LOADED REVOLVER and demanding that he or she be given some rental skis for the express purpose of suffering SERIOUS INJURY OR DEATH, leaving the rental personnel with NO CHOICE but to . . ." etc.

Okay! Now you're ready to "hit the slopes." Ski experts recommend that you start by taking a group lesson, because otherwise they would have to get real jobs. To start the lesson, your instructor, who is always a smiling 19-year-old named Chip, will take you to the top of the mountain and explain basic ski safety procedures until he feels that the cold has killed enough of your brain cells that you will cheerfully follow whatever lunatic command he gives you. Then he'll ski a short distance down the mountain, just to the point where it gets very steep, and swoosh to a graceful stop, making it look absurdly easy. It *is* absurdly easy for Chip, because underneath his outfit he's wearing an antigravity device. All the expert skiers wear them. You don't actually believe that "ski jumpers" can go off those ridiculously high ramps and just float to the ground unassisted without breaking into walnut-sized pieces, do you? Like Tinkerbell or something? Don't be a cretin.

After Chip stops, he turns to the group, his skis hovering as much as three inches above the snow, and orders the first student to copy what he did. This is the fun part.

Woodland creatures often wake up from hibernation just to watch this part, because even they understand that the laws of physics, which are strictly enforced on ski slopes, do not permit a person to simply stop on the side of a snow-covered mountain if his feet are encased in bowling balls attached to what are essentially large pieces of Teflon. Nevertheless, the first student, obeying Chip's command, cautiously pushes himself forward, and then, making an unusual throat sound, passes Chip at Warp Speed and proceeds on into the woods, flailing his arms like a volunteer in a highly questionable nerve-gas experiment.

"That was good!" shouts Chip, grateful that he is wearing waterproof fibers inasmuch as he will be wetting his pants repeatedly during the course of the lesson. Then he turns to the rest of the group and says, "Next!"

The group's only rational response, of course, would be to lie down in the snow and demand a rescue helicopter. But these are not rational beings; these are ski students. And so, one by one, they, too, ski into the woods, then stagger out, sometimes with branches sticking out, antler-like, from their foreheads, and do it *again*. "Bend your knees this time!" Chip advises, knowing that this will actually make them go *faster*. He loves his work.

Eventually, of course, you get better at it. If you stick with your lessons, you'll become an "intermediate" skier, meaning you'll learn to fall *before* you reach the woods. That's where I am now, in stark contrast to my 9-year-old son, who has not yet studied gravity in school and therefore became an expert in a matter of hours. Watching him flash effortlessly down the slope, I experience, as a parent, feelings of both pride and hope: pride in his accomplishment, and hope that someday, somehow, he'll ski near enough to where I'm lying that I'll be able to trip him with my poles.

IMPORTANT FINAL WORD OF ADVICE

Whatever sport you decide to become involved in, you should not plunge into it without first consulting with your physician. You can reach him on his cellular phone, in a dense group of trees, somewhere in the vicinity of the fourteenth hole.

12

YOUR AGING
PARENTS:
GETTING EVEN
WITH YOU
FOR TEETHING

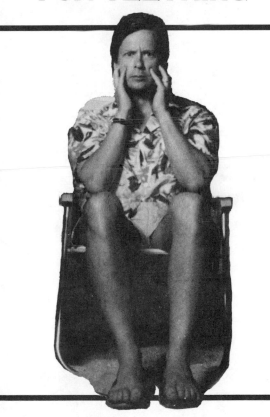

Back in the old days, most families were close-knit. Grown children and their parents continued to live together, under the same roof, sometimes in the same small, crowded room, year in and year out, until they died, frequently by strangulation.

No! Please excuse my cynical remark. Family life was wonderful back in those days, because there were no cars or televisions or microwave ovens or flush toilets or vaccines of any kind, plus there were wolves, so people really had to stick together. The family unit was organized according to what anthropologists call "The Beverly Hillbillies Principle," wherein the oldest member of the clan, played by Granny Clampett, had the most authority and received the most respect. In the evening the entire family would gather 'round and listen as this person handed down generations-old and oft-repeated stories of family history and lore:

GRANDMA: Tonight I think I'll hand down the oft-repeated story about how great-great-great-grandfather Lester bonked his head on the plow handle and then started dressing as a woman.

151

LITTLE BEATRICE: Oh shit, not again.

MAMA (whapping little Beatrice affectionately with the churn handle): You hush up and listen, child, or someday you'll be unable to inflict this particular wad of lore on *your* grandchildren.

GRANDMA: Well, it seems that one day, great-great-great-grandfather Lester set out toward the avocado field, and he AWWWKKKK

LITTLE BEN: Look! Grandma's being dragged off by a wolf!

PAPA: Big one, too. That's at least as big as the one that got Grandpa.

MAMA: Well, Uncle Webster, I guess *you're* the eldest in the family now!

UNCLE WEBSTER: I guess so! So it seems that one day great-great-great-grandfather Lester set out toward the avocado field . . .

And so it went, from generation to generation. Things are very different now. Members of your modern nuclear family do not spend a quiet evening together unless they are trapped in an elevator. And your modern young people do not view their elders as sources of wisdom. Our generation certainly didn't. We got all our wisdom from songs written by currently deceased rock stars whose bloodstreams contained the annual narcotics outputs of entire Third World nations. We viewed our parents as bizarre alien life-forms whose sole biological function was to provide us with money so we could go off and live in the geographically opposite end of the country. We deeply resented any effort by our parents to meddle in our lives: we were furious when they urged us to become dentists or—God forbid—lawyers, instead of pursuing careers in fields that we considered to be truly fulfilling and meaningful, such as zither repair; we were outraged when they questioned our decisions to get married to people we had known for only a few days and had never seen in direct sunlight.

And of course we were *really* annoyed at our parents when, a few years later, we got divorced and enrolled in law school.

But eventually there came a reconciliation. As we grew older and more mature, as we started having children of our own, we began to see our parents in a new light, to realize that they were not, really, so different from us, and that only they could provide us with something very precious, something that had been missing from our lives: reliable babysitting.

So most of us are spending at least some time with our parents again. But this is not easy. For one thing, your parents naturally have trouble accepting the fact that you are a genuine grownup. You may view yourself as a mature, self-reliant person, but your mom views you as a person who once got lost in the department store and got so scared that you pooped your pants, which caused you to become so ashamed that you tried to hide in the Ladies' Lingerie Department, where the nice clerk was able to find you because she noticed the highly unromantic aroma emanating from somewhere inside a rack of negligees. Likewise your dad still has occasional back pain related to the time you fell asleep on the Jungle Cruise ride at Disneyland and he had to carry you for the rest of the day, covering an estimated 450 miles. It's because of many vivid memories like this that, on a fundamental level of your parents' psyche, you're always three years old. Everything that has happened to you since infancy—puberty, marriage, career, parenthood— is just a temporary phase you're going through. This is why, even though you're the president of a large corporation with a personal helicopter and authority over thousands of people and millions of dollars, your mom still, automatically, when you leave her house, zips your jacket all the way up to your chin.

But while your parents continue to view you as the child you were in 1952, you're starting to notice definite changes in them. Your mom, for example, seems to be much more into cleanliness. She's no longer accustomed to having small children around. It's been years since she has discovered a large, unexplained deposit of hardened Zoo-Roni on the sofa. She has nice, unspoiled furniture now, and it has stayed nice for a long time, and when you visit her, especially with your kids, she becomes edgy. She gets the vacuum cleaner out a lot, trying to look casual about it, but definitely not comfortable, trailing along after the kids with the motor running. She'll cook an elaborate meal, but she won't eat any of it. She'll claim she's not hungry, as she prowls around the dining room on Full Crumb Alert, attempting to conceal the Dust Buster under her apron. "Don't mind me, you just go ahead and eat," she'll say, sometimes from under the table. You wind up using as many as four plates per meal because your mom keeps snatching them up and washing them between bites.

Your dad seems different, too. You remember him as a competent, authoritative, worldly guy, usually very busy, and now he schedules his entire day around "Wheel of Fortune." He repeats things a lot and his shirts look way too big and he doesn't know who won the World Series and when you go somewhere together you try to make sure it's in your car because he drives way below the speed limit and hits the brakes hard for everything, including mailboxes. Also, he and your mom have both become abnormally attached to some kind of pet, a dog or a cat that they got after all the kids left home. They buy it sweaters and birthday presents and they have conversations with it that are often longer and more meaningful than the ones they have with you.

So, as much as you love your parents, your relationship with them tends to be uneasy. It can get a lot worse if your parents reach the point where they can no longer completely care for themselves, and the roles are reversed and the authority figure in the relationship suddenly becomes you. Little Poopy Pants. You become impatient with your parents, and you catch yourself talking to them exactly the way you talk to your children: a little too loud, a little too slow, a little too simple.

If you'll forgive me, I'm not going to make any jokes about this particular aspect of getting older. I'm going to depart from my smartass tone, just briefly, to make the one serious statement I plan to make in this whole book, which is this: No matter how out-of-it your parents may seem to you, they're still your parents. They're not your children. They're going through something you've never gone through, and although you can probably help them with it, you are damned sure not an expert on it. I learned this, very painfully, a few years ago. I'll end this chapter with something I wrote at the time, for whatever good it does. Then I promise to go back to being irresponsible and vicious.

LOST IN AMERICA

My mother and I are driving through Hartford, Connecticut, on the way to a town called Essex. Neither of us has ever been to Essex, but we're both desperately hoping that my mother will want to live there.

She has been rootless for several months now, moving from son to son around the country, ever since she sold the house she had lived in for forty years, the house she raised us in, the house my father built. The house where he died, April 4, 1984. She would note the date each year on the calendar in the kitchen.

"Dave died, 1984," the note would say. "Come back, Dave."

The note for July 5, their anniversary, said: "Married Dave, 1942. Best thing that ever happened to me."

The house was too big for my mother to handle alone, and we all advised her to sell it. Finally she did, and she shipped all her furniture to Sunnyvale, California, where my brother Phil lived. Her plan was to stay with him until she found a place of her own out there.

Only she hated Sunnyvale. At first this seemed almost funny, even to her. "All my worldly goods," she would say, marveling at it, "are in a warehouse in Sunnyvale, California, which I hate." She always had a wonderful sense of absurdity.

After a while it didn't seem so funny. My mother left Sunnyvale to live for a while with my brother Sam, in San Francisco, and then with me, in Florida; but she didn't want to stay with us. What she wanted was a home.

What she really wanted was her old house back.

With my father in it.

Of course, she knew she couldn't have that, but when she tried to think of what else she wanted, her mind would just lock up. She started to spend a lot of time watching soap operas. "You have to get on with your life," I would tell her, in this new, parental voice I was developing when I talked to her. Dutifully, she would turn off the TV and get out a map of the United States, which I bought her to help her think.

"Maybe Boulder would be nice," she would say, looking at Colorado. "I was born near Boulder."

"Mom," I would say in my new voice. "We've talked about Boulder fifty times, and you always end up saying you don't really want to live there."

Chastened, she would look back at her map, but I could tell she wasn't really seeing it.

"You have to be realistic," I would say. The voice of wisdom.

When she and I had driven each other just about crazy, she went back out to California, and repeated the process with both of my brothers. Then one night she called to ask, very apologetically, if I would go with her to look at Essex, Connecticut, which she had heard was nice. It was a bad time for me, but of course I said yes, because your mom is your mom. I met her in Hartford and rented a car.

•   •   •

I'm driving; my mother is looking out the window. "I came through Hartford last year with Frank and Mil, on the way to Maine," she says. Frank was my father's brother; he has just died. My mother loved to see him. He reminded her of my father.

"We were singing," my mother says. She starts to sing:

"I'm forever blowing bubbles
Pretty bubbles in the air."

I can tell she wants me to sing, too. I know the words; we sang this song when I was little.

"First they fly so high, nearly reach the sky
Then like my dreams, they fade and die."

But I don't sing. I am all business.
"I miss Frank," says my mother.
Essex turns out to be a beautiful little town, and we look at two nice, affordable apartments. But I can tell right away that my mother doesn't want to be there. She doesn't want to say so, after asking me to fly up from Miami, but we both know.

The next morning, in the motel coffee shop, we have a very tense breakfast.

"Look, Mom," I say, "you have to make some kind of decision." Sounding very reasonable.

She looks down at her map. She starts talking about Boulder again. This sets me off. I lecture her, tell her she's being childish. She's looking down at her map, gripping it. I drive her back to Hartford, neither of us saying much. I put her on a plane; she's going to Milwaukee, to visit my dad's sister, then back to my brother in Sunnyvale, California. Which she hates.

The truth is, I'm relieved that she's leaving.

"You can't help her," I tell myself, "until she decides what she wants." It is a sound position.

About a week later, my wife and I get a card from my mother.

"This is to say happy birthday this very special year," it says. "And to thank you for everything."

Our birthdays are weeks away.

About two days later, my brother Phil calls, crying, from a hospital. My mother has taken a massive overdose of Valium and alcohol. The doctors want permission to turn off the machines. They say there's no hope.

We talk about it, but there really isn't much to say. We give the permission.

It's the only logical choice.

The last thing I saw my mother do, just before she went down the tunnel to her plane, was turn and give me a big smile. It wasn't a smile of happiness; it was the same smile I give my son when he gets upset listening to the news, and I tell him don't worry, we're never going to have a nuclear war.

I can still see that smile anytime I want. Close my eyes, and there it is. A mom, trying to reassure her boy that everything's going to be okay.

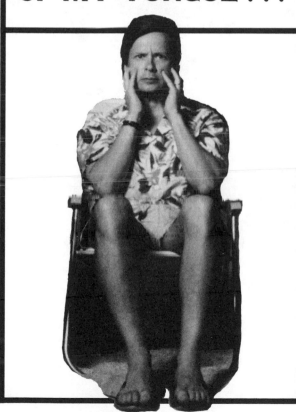

13

HOW TO COPE WITH . . . WITH . . . WAIT, IT'S RIGHT ON THE TIP OF MY TONGUE . . .

s you get older, you've probably noticed that you tend to forget things. You'll be talking with somebody at a party, and you'll *know* that you know this person, but no matter how hard you try, you can't remember his or her name. This can be very embarrassing, especially if he or she turns out to be your spouse.

The first few times you commit this kind of *faux pas* (literally, "hors d'oeuvre"), you tend to gloss it over. But eventually you start to worry, to wonder if maybe you could be coming down with Whatshisname's Disease. Well, let me offer you these kind words of gentle reassurance: Don't be such a moron. The odds are that you're merely suffering from a very common middle-aged-person condition known technically to medical professionals as "having a brain cluttered up with useless crap left over from thirty years ago." For example, to this very day I can remember the words and tune to an incredibly irritating song sung long ago by Annette Funicello called "Pineapple Princess."

I hated this song when it came out. I still hate this song. I favor the death penalty for whoever wrote it. So naturally my brain has assigned it Priority One Status and placed it on a special E-Z Access Memory Circuit, which means that whenever I'm trying desperately to remember the name of the party hostess, or where I left my car keys, or how old I am, there's old Annette, yammering away in the forefront of my brain lobes.

And if I manage to mentally shove "Pineapple Princess" out of the way, my memory, always looking to help me out, alertly provides me with: a cigarette commercial jingle from 1959. Of *course!* The very thing I need! While I'm nearing panic at the shopping mall, racking my brain, trying to remember whether I had my son with me when I left home, it is very convenient that my brain is shrieking:

> *Every Parliament gives you . . .*
> *EXTRA MARGIN!*
> *The filter's recessed and made to stay*
> *A neat, clean quarter-inch away!*

Of course, your brain doesn't remember *everything* from your youth. Your brain shrewdly elects to remember only the truly *useless* things. This is why you can no longer do long division, but you remember the name of the kid who ate the worm in third grade (Charlie Ringwold). When I was in high school I read large wads of Shakespeare, but all I can quote is:

> *To be, or not to be, that is the question.*
> *Whether 'tis something something, etc.*
> *And alas poor Yorick doesn't look so good either.*

Whereas I will go to my grave being able to recite
flawlessly:

I'm a choice M&Ms peanut
Fresh-roasted to a golden tan,
Drenched in creamy milk chocolate,
And covered with a thin candy shell.

Is that pathetic, or what? And I'm not alone. If you
surveyed a hundred typical middle-aged Americans, I
bet you'd find that only two of them could tell you their
blood types, but every last one would know the theme
song from "The Beverly Hillbillies." Right? Even as you
read these words, your brain, which cannot remember
more than two words of your wedding vows, is cheerfully
singing:

Come and listen to my story 'bout a man named Jed,
A poor mountaineer barely kept his fam'ly fed . . .

What can you do about this useless brain clutter? Unfortunately, the only known cure is a painful medical
procedure wherein doctors drill a hole in your skull so
the stored-up information can escape. If the patient is a
middle-aged man, the doctors have to leap out of the way
to avoid being hit by a high-pressure blast of numbers
such as the batting averages for the entire Toronto Blue
Jays lineup for 1979 and all the other vital pieces of
information that guys tend to remember in lieu of trivia
such as the full names of their children. The main draw-

back with this procedure is that if the doctors don't plug up your skull hole in time, you can lose your entire brain contents and wind up as a pathetic drooling cretin with no hope for meaningful employment outside of the state legislature.

So you're probably better off just learning how to cope with your memory problem. Sometimes you can cover it up by means of clever techniques such as the one suggested by famous etiquette expert Marjabelle Young Stewart in her book, *The New Etiquette.* She suggests that, in situations where people are having trouble remembering names, the ticket is for somebody to just step forward and introduce himself. As Marjabelle Young Stewart puts it:

> If you say "I'm Joshua Wright," the other person invariably responds with, "I'm Sally Jones," and the introductions are accomplished, at no loss of face to anyone.

There! It couldn't be simpler! Of course, some of you are saying, "But what if my name *isn't* Joshua Wright?" The answer is—and I'm sure I speak for Marjabelle Young Stewart as well as many other famous etiquette experts when I say this—tough shit. Because sometimes, for etiquette's sake, we have to tell "little white lies," such as when we tell a friend we're sorry that her cat died even though the truth is we would cheerfully have thrust the vicious little hairball into the trash compactor ourselves if we ever could have gotten our hands on it. It just so happens that, in social situations, it's easier for everybody involved if you agree to be "Joshua Wright" and the other person agrees to be "Sally Jones," unless of course the other person is the Pope, in which case you would refer to him as "Your Holiness Sally Jones."

Another memory aid that is recommended by leading memory experts is to use a "mnemonic device." Let's say you want to remember that a certain business associate is named Ralph. Here's how a mnemonic device could help:

YOU: I don't know! I swear it!
LEADING MEMORY EXPERT: Perhaps if we increased the Mnemonic Device to *650 volts* . . .
YOU: RALPH!! HIS NAME IS RALPH!!!

So you see that there's no reason why you can't lead a normal and highly productive life despite the fact that your brain has turned into a festering dumpster of informational waste. In the next chapter we'll explore yet another exciting facet of the aging process, the name of which escapes me at the moment.

14

AGING
GRACELESSLY:
THE JOYS OF
GEEZERHOOD

The central point of this final chapter is that—follow my logic carefully here—unless you die, you will continue to get older. (It's insights like this that separate the professional book author from the person with a real job.)

Of course, we can't say exactly *how* old you're going to get without knowing certain scientific facts about you, such as your genetic makeup, your medical history, and your tendency to wager large sums of money with men named "Snake." But if you pick up any current actuarial table and look up the average life span for a person of your particular age, sex, and weight, you'll realize that, statistically, you have to squint like hell to read the numbers. This proves that you're *already* older than you think. And it's just going to get worse, because of a law of physics discovered by Albert Einstein, the brilliant physicist who not only invented the White Guy Afro haircut, but also discovered the Theory of Decade Relativity, which states: "Each decade goes exactly twice as fast as the decade before." This is why so much more seemed to happen in the sixties than in the seventies, and why your only truly enduring memory of the eighties, when all is said and done, will be Tammy Faye Bakker.

So now here we are in the nineties, which means that regardless of how many gallons of Oil of Olay you smear on yourself, you're going to start aging faster than a day-old bagel in a hot dumpster. You need to think about this. You need to decide how you're going to deal with the fact that you're becoming an Older Person.

One way is to deny it. This is the Peter Pan approach, and it has a powerful appeal. Remember when you were a kid, and you saw the legendary TV musical version of *Peter Pan,* and Peter was striding around the stage declaring, "I WON'T grow up!"? Remember what you thought, in your innocent, naïve, trusting childlike way? You thought: *"That's* not a little boy. That's obviously middle-aged actress Mary Martin making a fool out of herself."

So we see that although age-denial is appealing, it can generally make a person look ridiculous. Oh, some people try to get away with it, the best example being the Rolling Stones. As I write these words, the remaining non-deceased Stones, some of whom were born during the Hundred Years War, are still out there on tour, still rockin' and rollin' and putting on an electrifying act that reaches its exciting climax during "Satisfaction," when drummer Charlie Watts hurls his dentures into the crowd.

But is this really working, even for the Stones? To find out, I went to see them when they came to Miami. I'd seen them once before, when we were all a *lot* younger, back in the sixties. That was one of those classic sixties rock concerts, the kind where even the police dogs were stoned, and where the show would be scheduled to start at 9:00 P.M., but nothing would happen until maybe 11:30, when one of the promoters would get up on stage and announce that there would be a slight delay because the band was still at the airport in New Zealand.

The concert I saw in Miami was very different. For one thing, it started on time, probably because if it hadn't, one of the estimated 13,000 attorneys in the audience would have filed a lawsuit. Also it was a much older crowd, a lot of middle-aged soft-rockers like myself, stylishly decked out in our casual-wear beepers, taking bold swigs of Diet Pepsi. Sure, some of us were high, but it was not so much the high of ingesting hallucinogenic substances as the high of knowing that you had a babysitter on a weekday night.

But the most striking difference, for me, was in the Stones themselves. I had remembered them as awesome, larger-than-life, near-mystical figures, so I was filled with anticipation when, two decades later, I took my seat high in the upper deck of the Orange Bowl in Miami. My excitement mounted as the stadium darkened, and the giant speakers started playing dramatic buildup music, and clouds of smoke poured onto the stage. And then, when the crowd was about to explode with excitement, there was a blinding flash of light, and we heard the slashing, driving opening guitar riff of "Start Me Up," and suddenly, out of the darkness, came . . . these *little teeny* Rolling Stones. Maybe 14 inches tall. Talk about your comical letdowns. They looked like the Decadent Rock Band Action Figure Set from Toys "Я" Us.

I realize that this impression was partly due to the altitude of my seat, but it also had something to do with getting older. It's one thing when you're 19 and unemployed and mad at the world, and the the Stones are these godlike outlaw rebels; but it's a whole different thing when you have a family and a mortgage and disability insurance, and the Stones have become essentially a corporation whose members are the same average age as the justices of the U.S. Supreme Court. I still enjoyed their music, but watching them strut around down there, smallish, aging men preening in their pants purchased at the Rock-'n'-Roll Superstar Extremely Tight Clothing Outlet, I couldn't help but think that they looked a little bit—this is difficult for me to write, about the Stones—silly.

Of course, I'd act silly too, if somebody was paying me millions of dollars. But nobody is, which is exactly my point. There's still a market demand for Mick and the boys to act the way they they acted twenty-five years ago. But there is zero demand for the rest of us to do this, and if we try, we look silly, and we don't get paid for it. So I'm recommending against trying to deny the aging process, unless you're a Certified Rolling Stone. If you're a Certified Public Accountant, you have to accept the fact that you're not going to suddenly transform yourself into a the vibrant, youthful person you once were by getting a snake tattooed on your butt. You're going to transform yourself into a Certified Public Accountant with a snake on his butt, and you're going to feel stupid when you visit your proctologist.

So how *should* you cope with the fact that you're getting older? One approach, taken by millions of people, is to age gracefully, to enjoy the serenity that the golden years can bring, with their gifts of maturity and wisdom.

Or you can turn into a crusty old fart. This is definitely my plan. I figure that one of the major advantages of getting old is that you're allowed, even expected, to be eccentric and crotchety and just generally weird. Why not take advantage of this? Older people, if they play their cards right, can get away with almost anything.

The all-time example of this is, of course, Ronald Reagan. Here's a man who was twice elected to the most powerful position on Earth despite needing a Tele-PrompTer to correctly identify what year it was. But no matter how out-of-it he seemed to be, the people loved him. It was as if we were in an airplane, and the pilot got sick, so our kindly old Uncle Bob had to take the controls. We didn't *expect* as much from President Uncle Bob. We considered it a major triumph if he didn't crash.

Remember how he handled the Iran-contra Never-Ending Scandal from Hell? He went on national television, the President of the United States, and said it wasn't his fault, because *he was not aware, at the time, of what his foreign policy was.* In fact he had to appoint a Distinguished Commission to *find out* what his foreign policy was, and report back to him.

Now if he'd been a *young* President, some little Mister Competence right-on-top-of-everything jogging fact-spouting pissant whippersnapper like Jimmy Carter, his own *wife* would have called for his impeachment. But with Ronald Reagan, the voters, who also have never had the vaguest idea what our foreign policy was, were very forgiving. "Yeah," they said. "How's he supposed to remember *every darned time* he authorizes the sale of weapons to enemy nations? Why don't you medias leave him alone?!" And Ron went right on grinning and being popular and pretty much limiting his executive actions to signing stuff and having polyps removed until the end of his wildly successful term in office.

But an older person doesn't have to be the President to get away with things. I once knew a very sharp elderly lady who used to amuse herself, at parties, by trapping people's feet with her cane. She'd sidle up next to a victim, looking sweet and harmless and out-of-it, and she'd plant her cane tip right on the victim's shoe top and lean on it. The victim, not wishing to embarrass her, would say nothing while trying, subtly, to work his foot free, but as soon as he did, she'd shift over a little bit and harpoon him again. This would go on for fifteen minutes, the two of them moving around the room in a hilarious silent dance. It made for fine entertainment, and a younger person could never have pulled it off.

A certified geezer is also freer to express displeasure. Once I was walking in midtown Manhattan at rush hour, and I came to a massive traffic jam, horns honking everywhere, and right in the middle of a major intersection, the center of the whole mess, was a taxi driver honking at a very elderly man who was standing directly in front of the cab, blocking its path, and hitting it with his umbrella.

WHAP the umbrella would go, on the hood. Then, very slowly, the elderly man would raise it into the air, over his head, where it would waver for a second and then . . .

WHAP it would come down on the hood again. I stopped to watch, along with a large crowd of New Yorkers, who have an inbred genetic hatred of taxi drivers and who cheered louder with every WHAP. Nobody made any effort to move the elderly man out of the way. He was doing exactly what we'd all wanted to do a million times, but we couldn't because we'd get run over or arrested. I finally had to leave, but I like to think that the reason New York traffic is always so screwed up is that the elderly man is still in that intersection, whapping away.

So for my money, geezerhood is definitely the way to go. In fact, you might want to start practicing right now.

HOW TO GEEZE

Fashion Men should wear hats at all times, including in the bath. They should always have their top shirt button buttoned, but not necessarily all of the lower ones. For a casual summer look, men should wear a comfort-inducing, armpit-revealing sleeveless undershirt, Bermuda shorts, and—this is *very* important—black knee socks with wingtipped shoes. Women should wear a "house dress" large enough to cover an actual house. It should always be the same one, and it should be worn everywhere, including to the beach and funerals. Women should also give their hair a very natural and pleasing look by dying it exactly the same color as a radioactive carrot.

Dealing With Your Children and Grandchildren When they come to see you, spend the entire time complaining to them about how they never come to see you.

Driving The geezer car should be as large as possible. If a fighter jet can't land on it, you don't want to drive it. If necessary, you should get *two* cars and have them welded together. You should grip the wheel tightly enough so that you cannot be detached from it without a surgical procedure, and you should sit way down in the seat so that you're looking directly ahead at the speedometer. You should select a speed in advance—23 miles per hour is very popular—and drive this speed at all times, regardless of whether you're in your driveway or on the interstate. Always come to a full stop when you notice a Potentially Hazardous Road Condition such as an intersection or a store or a sidewalk or a tree. If you're planning to make a turn at any point during the trip, you should plan ahead by putting your blinker on as soon as you start the car. Never park the car without making a minimum of seventeen turns.

Announcing Your Intimate Medical Problems This is an excellent way to make new friends, especially in restaurants. "I can't eat that spicy food," you should announce to nobody in particular in a voice loud enough to direct military field operations. "I got this armpit cyst the size of a regulation softball, and that spicy food plays hell with it. One time I was eating chili and, bang, the damn thing *exploded,* and there was cyst contents flying *every-where,* you had people diving under tables and . . . Hey!

How come everybody's leaving? Can I have your egg roll?"

And so on. You get the idea. The main thing is, *don't be discreet.* We Boomers have never been a discreet generation, and I see no reason why we should fade quietly away just because we're getting old. Let's not go out with a whimper. Let's go out proudly whapping the umbrella of defiance on the taxicab hood of time. Let's remember the words of that rock song from the sixties, the anthem of our entire generation, the unforgettable song that spoke for all of us when it said . . . when it said . . . ummm . . .

Jeez, how the hell *did* that song go?